Alfred John Morris

The shepherd and his lambs

or, Chapters and songs on all the Scriptures that connect together Christ and

children

Alfred John Morris

The shepherd and his lambs
or, Chapters and songs on all the Scriptures that connect together Christ and children

ISBN/EAN: 9783741189937

Manufactured in Europe, USA, Canada, Australia, Japa

Cover: Foto ©ninafisch / pixelio.de

Manufactured and distributed by brebook publishing software (www.brebook.com)

Alfred John Morris

The shepherd and his lambs

CHAPTER I

JESUS, A CHILD.

Acts iv. 30.—"THY HOLY CHILD JESUS."

I WISH to speak to children about Jesus Christ; and what the Bible says Jesus Christ has spoken and done respecting children.

Jesus Christ is the greatest, wisest, holiest, kindest being that ever appeared in the world; and it is very right that children should care to know what he thinks of them, and what he is able and willing to do for them.

I have often heard children say, when a stranger has been coming on a visit to the house, "Does he like children?" because this would make them feel at home with him; but if he did not like children, they might be afraid of him, especially if he was a great and strong man, or very learned, or very rich and grand.

Now I wish to show that Jesus Christ likes children, and that he says so himself. And I wish to point out *how* he likes them, and *why* he likes them; and how

B

much he has done, and is willing to do, to *prove* that
he likes them.   And may what I say do you good "in
the name of the holy child Jesus."

In this chapter I shall consider two things; that
Jesus Christ *was once himself a child;* and *why he
became one.*

FIRST, THEN, JESUS CHRIST WAS ONCE A CHILD.

What year is this?   *Eighteen hundred and sixty-
eight.*   What does that mean?   Why, that all those
years have passed since Jesus Christ was born.   People
who love Jesus Christ, and do what he bids them,
think that his birth was the greatest thing that ever
happened in the world; and so they reckon time
from it.   Before Christ was born, men reckoned time
from the beginning of time, that is, from the creation
of the world.   But after Christ was born, those who
thought a great deal of him, more of him than all
other men, reckoned time from his birth.   You often
see two large letters, A.D., put before the year.   They
are the first letters of two Latin words which mean,
in the year of the Lord; that is, in the year of Jesus
Christ, there having been so many years since he
came into the world.

Well, all that time ago, nearly two thousand years
ago, Jesus Christ began life in this world as a baby.
I say, "in this world," because the Bible tells us that

he was alive before he came into this world. Other men are not alive before they come into this world. You and I were nothing at all till we were born. We *began to be* when we were born. But Jesus Christ was "the Son of God" before he became "the Son of man." John the Baptist said of him, "He was before me;" though John was born several months before him. And Jesus Christ says of himself to the Jews, "Before Abraham was, I am." And there are many places in the Bible where he is said to have lived in great glory before man was made, or angels either. Indeed, he is said to have made all things and all beings. His name is "Emanuel, God with us."

But nearly two thousand years ago Jesus Christ *appeared* in the world. That is, in some way that we do not understand, he joined himself to our nature, to flesh and blood, as a babe. He came in the line of King David, and so is called "the offspring of David;" but his parents were in humble life. His father was a carpenter, and he himself is called a carpenter. For the Jews had a very good plan of bringing up their children to a trade. They said that the man who did not teach his child a trade brought him up to be a thief. And there was much truth in the saying, for men must live somehow, and, as Dr. Watts sings,

Satan finds some mischief still
For idle hands to do.

Now it was known beforehand, that Jesus Christ would come into the world. I don't say that people knew how he would come, or what exactly he would do when he did come : but God had taught many good men long before to speak and write about a great person, a glorious king, who should appear in the world. David and Daniel, Isaiah and Micah, and other men, had predicted, that is, *said before*, that he would come.

The Evangelists tell us that all *the rites of the law of Moses* were observed in the case of the child Jesus. He was circumcised on the eighth day, and he was presented in the temple when about six weeks old. By circumcision Jewish males were admitted into the Jewish church. It was a way of saying that none were too young to be connected with God and religion. And the presentation of the first-born in the temple was a saying that the first-born belonged to God ; and not only the first-born, but all children. It was common to offer God first-things of various kinds, and it meant that all the things in those kinds were his. All children are God's, and cannot too early give themselves to him. Until they can do that of their own will, it is the duty and privilege of their parents to do it for them in every possible way, especially by prayer and dedication.

WHY DID JESUS CHRIST BECOME A CHILD?

Every wise man has reasons for what he does : only foolish men act without knowing why they act. We may be sure that in doing so great a thing as coming into our world, Jesus Christ had very good reasons.

The Apostle Paul tells us in very few words Christ's object in coming. He "came into the world to save sinners." You have read of persons being drowned, and of other persons taking off their clothes and going into the water to prevent them being drowned. So Jesus Christ put off his glory, and came into our miserable and sinful world to save us.

Many things had to be done to save us, and Jesus Christ did them all.

He came that he might be able to *teach* man. In the first chapter of John's Gospel, Jesus Christ is called *God's Word*. "In the beginning was the Word, and the Word was with God, and the Word was God." You know what a word is; it is so many letters or sounds that tell what a person thinks or wishes. Words are our chief means of letting one another know our minds. If we had no words, we should find it very hard to hold any intercourse, to teach, to buy and sell, or indeed to do anything. Well, God had a great deal that he wanted to say to man, and Jesus Christ became his word. That is, as John

tells us, " the Word was made flesh, and dwelt among
us, (and we beheld his glory, the glory as of the only
begotten of the Father,) full of grace and truth." *He*
was "full of truth." Not only did he *speak* truth,
but he *was* truth. " I am the truth." Especially the
truth about God ; what God *is*, what God *means*,
what God *does*. " The only begotten Son, which is in
the bosom of the Father, he hath declared him. '
When you see Jesus Christ, read his life and death,
and notice how true and good, and holy and loving, he
was, you see God in a human being. The character
and words of Jesus, his actions and sufferings, " shew
us the Father."

You know that if you speak to people you must use
words which they understand. If a man talks to a
child, it is of no use to speak long words and great
thoughts. He must try to look at things in the way
in which a child looks at them, and speak of them as
a child speaks of them. And when God wished to
show men what he was, he sent his Son to be a man,
that men might learn through him what he was.
Christ is God's word in the flesh.

But Jesus Christ became a child that he might
be able to *feel with us*. Most people are afraid of God.
He is so great and strong and wise that they don't
think he cares for them, that he notices them, or has
any interest in their affairs. Heathens, that is, people

who had no knowledge of the true God, used to think that he did not trouble himself with men's doings and concerns, that they were beneath him. And we are all backward to feel that God is very near and very kind to us. Now the Bible teaches us that God *feels for us* like a father or a mother. And it goes farther: it says that Jesus Christ came into the world that he might *feel with us*. There is a great difference between feeling *for* people and feeling *with* them. It is the difference between kindness and sympathy. We cannot feel much with people unless we are or have been in their case. It is therefore the sufferers who feel with the suffering; the poor who feel with the poor; the sick who feel with the sick. Now, Jesus Christ, says Paul, is "touched with the feeling of our infirmities because he was tempted in all points like as we are." He knows what it is to be hungry and thirsty, and weary, and solitary, and full of pain, and tempted by the devil.

Is it not pleasant to think of him in this way? This was one reason why he became poor, because there are more poor people than rich ones in the world. And this was one reason why he became a child, because all people are children sometime. He feels with the poor, and with children.

My dear children, the Son of God knows what it is to be a child, to think as a child, to speak as a child, to understand as a child, to feel as a child. As a child he lay upon his mother's lap, and looked up smilingly into his mother's face. As a child he had his childish games, and shed his childish tears. As a child he had to put up with little troubles, and was sometimes vexed with naughty companions, and found his lessons sometimes hard, and met with many things he could not understand. And he remembers all this, and can enter into the feelings of little children, and cares much for them. *Think of Jesus Christ as a child*, and remember that he sees you, knows you, and feels with you. He became a child that he might do so.

Jesus Christ became a child that he might *do us good*, more good than any one else ever did or could do. We owe a great deal to our dear parents, and to kind friends, and to wise teachers; but we owe far more to Jesus Christ. They have saved us from ignorance and sickness and want and death; but Jesus came to save us from *sin*, and *Satan*, and *hell*. "Thou shalt call his name Jesus: for he shall save his people from their sins."

You are aware that when men try to do a great deal of good to other men, they must often put up with much pain and hardship. They must give up time and money and ease. They must make what are called "sacrifices." You cannot do much good in

this world without them. It is with good done as
it is with things bought; what is cheapest is of
smallest worth. All the best things cost the most.
And to give the best blessings to men costs much.

Some go through much trouble and difficulty in
order to do good to the ignorant and miserable and
wicked. They go to places very sad to see, and mix
with people whose lives and words are very bad, and
labour very hard. Some men go abroad, and become
in many things *like those* they wish to benefit. They
learn their languages, live with them, dress like them,
and all to make them feel at home, and convince them
that they are really loved, and get the means of
teaching them and making them feel.

Jesus Christ did this, only he did more than others
ever did. *They* have gone into strange places to do
good; *he* came into *a world* to do good. *They* have
put themselves into painful circumstances; *he* entered
a suffering nature. *They* have sometimes died to
benefit the lost; *he* became a mortal man that he
might be able to die for men.

I hope you see how much God must have loved us
to send Jesus Christ into our world as a child, to grow
up to be a man, and then to die for men. "God so
loved the world that he gave his only begotten Son,
that whosoever believeth in him should not perish but
have everlasting life."

"Only begotten Son." You know how dreadfully parents feel when they lose a child. And when they have but *one child*, and that dies, their trouble is greater than any words can speak. Indeed, in the Bible, sorrow for the loss of "an only child" is spoken of as the deepest sorrow. "They shall mourn for him as one that mourneth for an only son." Well, God of his own accord gave *his* only Son, Jesus Christ, for us. He gave him up to pain and shame and death. He gave him up for the sake of "the ungodly," for the sake of "sinners," for the sake of "enemies." How much he must have loved us!

This is why Jesus Christ became a child. We were very sinful and far from God, and he could not take any pleasure in us; and Jesus Christ, by his life and death, brings us near to God, makes us God's dear children, and God loves us now, and takes us home to heaven at death.

Was it not worth Christ's while to become a child ? And did it not show very great love ?

JESUS, A CHILD.

He might have come in glory bright,
   Upon a throne of cloud,
Wearing a crown of dazzling light,
   And speaking thunder-loud.

But he was born a little child,
   And weak as children are,
On whom his mother fondly smiled,
   And watched with mothers' care.

And thus he came that he might bless
   Our childhood's little years ;
Might learn to feel for its distress,
   And brighten up its tears.

And though he is in heaven to-day,
   He feels for children still ;
Hears all the little prayers they say,
   And both *can* help, and *will*.

CHAPTER II

THE CHILD JESUS AND THE INFANTS OF BETHLEHEM.

Matthew ii. 16. — "THEN HEROD, WHEN HE SAW THAT HE WAS MOCKED OF THE WISE MEN, WAS EXCEEDING WROTH, AND SENT FORTH, AND SLEW ALL THE CHILDREN THAT WERE IN BETHLEHEM, AND IN ALL THE COASTS THEREOF, FROM TWO YEARS OLD AND UNDER, ACCORDING TO THE TIME WHICH HE HAD DILIGENTLY INQUIRED OF THE WISE MEN."

THE birth of Jesus was the greatest thing that ever took place. It was greater than the birth of the wisest, or strongest, or best man that ever lived. And it made a great stir in both heaven and earth. Angels rejoiced in it. And so did men. Good men in Judæa were very glad of it. And wise men came from a long way off to do honour to the child Jesus.

But perhaps nothing ever took place which was looked at in exactly the same way by all persons. Perhaps nothing joyful ever took place that did not make some one sorry ; and perhaps nothing good ever took place that some did not make a bad use of. While holy angels, and Simeon and Anna, and the wise men, and many more, " rejoiced with exceeding great joy," there were bad people in Judæa who were

very sorry because of Christ's birth, and would have
given anything to prevent it. And they tried to put
Christ to death.

NOTICE WHAT WAS DONE TO KILL JESUS.

There was a king in Judæa called "Herod the
Great." Those who admired him gave him that name.
He was not truly great. He was a bold and clever
man, and rose to power by all sorts of art and wickedness. Bold and clever people often get on in this
world ; and the reason is, because there are so many
weak and foolish people to fear and flatter them.

Herod was great in sin. He was a great usurper,
a great tyrant, a great murderer. I should not like
to tell you *how* bad he was, if I could. He never
stopped at anything that would help his selfish ends,
or please his wicked passions. He murdered his own
sons, and his own wife ; and you may think how poor
a chance other people would have with him. And
yet, he was once a little smiling babe, and was dandled
and kissed by a fond mother. When you see a child,
you can never tell what it will be when it becomes a
man. Some believe that when Cain was born, Eve
thought he was the promised seed. What a mistake !

This bad man wished to kill Jesus Christ. He was
afraid of him. He heard that a child was born who

would be "King of the Jews." At this time the
Jews were expecting the coming of a great person
who would reign over them, the person spoken of in
the Old Testament, who should rule men justly, and
put down what was wrong. And Herod was afraid
that this child was the one meant, and that he would
bring his own wicked reign to an end. And so he
wished to get him out of the way.

In order to do this, he tried to find out the *place*
and the *time* of Christ's birth, but in a quiet and secret
way, that it might not lead to any disturbance. And
he pretended that he wished to know for the purpose
of honouring Jesus. Even men of great power have
sometimes to take care that they do not offend other
people. It would be a dreadful thing if bad men had
it all their own way in this world. How pleasant it
is to think that the only being that has *all power* is
the only being who never does wrong. *God* means
good.

Herod could not do as he wished, and so he did as
he could. He had made up his mind to have Jesus
killed, and therefore he ordered all the infants in
Bethlehem under two years of age to be destroyed,
making sure that Jesus would be one of them. We
are not told how many there were; but in a little
place like Bethlehem, there could not be very many
so young; and some of them would perhaps be hid.

However, Herod was such a monster, that to save himself he would not have minded how many children or men either he killed.

It was a dreadful thing for the parents of these children. Perhaps the lives of some were "bound up" in their children's lives. And Matthew applies to it some very sorrowful words which had been used by one of the prophets. "Then was fulfilled that which was spoken by Jeremy the prophet, saying, In Rama was there a voice heard, lamentation, and weeping, and great mourning, Rachel weeping for her children, and would not be comforted, because they are not."

But Jesus was not among them. There was an eye looking on which no one could see. The Father of Jesus knew what Herod wished, and would try to do; and he warned the wise men in a dream to go home without telling Herod anything; and he warned Joseph to take Jesus away out of danger, till Herod was dead. And Herod did die, a horrible death, as horrible a death as could be; and Jesus lived to be king both of Jews and Gentiles, and he is reigning in great glory to-day. Oh! how blessed it is to have God for our friend, who knows everything about us; and knows what others do to us, or would like to do to us; and is able to prevent them doing us any harm. There is one who would, if he could, destroy us, Satan,

Herod's father and king, and the father and king of all who are like Herod; but God knows all the "depths of Satan," and can defend us from his hatred. "Hell and destruction are before the Lòrd; how much more the hearts of the children of men ?"

WHAT MAY WE LEARN FROM ALL THIS ?

We may learn something from it as to *the great wickedness which may belong to men*. To put a number of innocent children to death in this way showed as bad a heart as a man could have. They had done no harm to Herod, or to any one else. And he knew that it would shock and sadden many times as many of near relatives. They were, as they have since been called, "Innocents"—innocent of all offence against God or man. No man could have killed them who was not full of himself, who had not made a god of himself. But when men get to love themselves more than all besides, they are ready to do anything to gain their ends. Take care you are not selfish. Selfishness is sin, is Satan. Love is of God. "God is love."

Men do not become as bad as Herod *all at once*. I dare say that when Herod was a child, he would have wept over such a story as that of Bethlehem. But the heart gets hardened by sin. Living in sin is like running down a hill; you go faster and faster. Sin is like a child, small and weak at first; but it gets greater and stronger until it must have its own way ; and then the sinner is lost. When children put off good things to a future day, they are making it harder for them ever to attend to them. If you had a nasty poisonous weed in your garden, would you do all you could to make it grow, and think to cut it down when it had got as large as it could get, and had done as much mischief as it could do ?

We may learn from this killing of the infants, *how little children may suffer in this world.* Though they have not sinned, yet they suffer. They suffer death. They may suffer even a violent death, a death which ought only to come to great criminals. And you see, too, how *some may suffer because of others.* These infants were destroyed because another child was born. And very often children suffer because other people have done wrong ; or because they are connected with people who have done wrong.

Now this is a sad thing ; and sometimes it is asked, Why does God allow it ? Why does he let those who have done no wrong be punished, and sometimes instead of those who have done wrong ? Why does he let children come into the world to be treated as many are treated, to live lives of pain, and die before they have been of any use in the world ? I can't tell all God's reasons ; but we must remember that God may

c

have good reasons for what he does, *though we do not know them.* And, also, that he can *make it all right in the other world.*

These little children have been called martyrs. They were not *really* martyrs, because a martyr is one who *chooses* to suffer for Christ, and they did not choose to do it. But they were the first whose blood was shed for Christ's sake. And Jesus Christ has long ago made it up to them. They are all in heaven, and they are more happy there than if they had died a natural death.

But the greatest thing we may learn is this, that *good things may be made bad things, and the best things may be made the worst things, by the badness which is in man.*

Nothing could be better than the birth of Jesus ; and yet Herod turned it into a curse. It was a thing to make men glad ; and yet it became the cause of sorrow and woe to many families. It was "glad tidings of great joy ;" and yet it filled many eyes with tears, and many mouths with lamentations. It was to bring "peace and goodwill," and yet it moved Herod's bad passions, and led him to shed innocent blood. It was not the fault of Christ's birth, but of Herod's evil heart, which made a bad use of Christ's birth.

Now something of this kind is always going on.

Good things take place every day which our sins make bad. God puts many cups of joy into our hands, and our sins mix bitterness and poison with them. Even the birth of God's only begotten Son was the reason why the infants of Bethlehem were slaughtered, because a bad king was afraid of losing his throne.

We may make a bad use of Christ's birth. It may be better for us that *he* had never been born. And it will be, if, now that he has come, *we do not receive him*. Simeon said of him, "Behold, this child is set for the fall and rising again of many in Israel." And many *souls* have *fallen* by rejecting him, as many souls have risen by receiving him.

When Jesus sent out the seventy disciples, he told them to say, when any city received them, "The kingdom of God is come nigh unto you." And he told them also, when any city refused to receive them, to say the same thing, "Be ye sure of this, that the kingdom of God is come nigh unto you." You see the very same thing might be both good and bad. It was good as Christ meant it, it might be bad as men made it.

It is awful to think that many, through their own fault, will have to curse the day of Christ's birth! Let all that read these lines take care they are not among them!

THE CHILD JESUS AND THE INFANTS OF BETHLEHEM.

Why those groans, that awful shrieking ?
  What hath cursed those happy homes ?
Mothers' hearts are well nigh breaking
  For their infants' bloody dooms.

What have infants done to bring
  On their heads so fierce a ban ?
Have they harmed the cruel king,
  Or offended God or man ?

Herod hears the people say,
  Christ is born, foretold of yore,
And, to take his life away,
  Takes the lives of fifty more.

Thus so soon did man begin
  E'en to make the Christ a curse ;
And to all who live in sin,
  He may still be death, and worse.

Lord, my heart would welcome thee,
  Though the world should hate and scorn ;
Be thou born again in me,
  Make me glad that thou wast born !

CHAPTER III

THE CHILDHOOD OF JESUS CHRIST.

Luke ii. 52.—"AND JESUS INCREASED IN WISDOM AND STATURE, AND IN FAVOUR WITH GOD AND MAN."

YOU perhaps have sometimes wished you knew more about Jesus Christ as a child. It is natural for children to wish so. I have often wished so myself. I should like to have seen him at home, and at play, and among his little companions. I should like to know what he said, whether he was merry or grave, whether he took an interest in things that please most children.

In the beginning of the Gospel, what may be called the childhood of the Church of Jesus Christ, there were many books written which pretended to give an account of Jesus Christ, besides the four Gospels which we have. And some of these sham Gospels said many things about the childhood of Jesus, foolish stories of what he said and did when an infant. Some of these were called "The Gospel of the Infancy:" but they are so silly, and so unlike the true Gospels of

Matthew, Mark, Luke, and John, that any one can see that they are not true.   But they show, and this is why I mention them, how natural it is for people to wish to know more about Christ's childhood.

We have very little about it in the New Testament. Until he was thirty years old we read nothing of his words or actions but his appearance in the temple on one occasion, which I shall speak to you of by itself. Why is this?   Why have we scarcely anything about the childhood, and nothing about the youth, of Jesus? The cause is, that childhood and youth are seasons in which people are to *prepare* to speak and act, rather than to do them.   Solomon says "there is a time to plant."   Now, when people are young, that is the time to plant with them.   I mean, to plant their minds and hearts with the seeds of wise thoughts and good feelings; and when they grow up, that is the time to reap. We can't expect fruit in the spring : we must wait till the summer and autumn.   The early years of life are very important to the young, and so is what they think and do very important to them also; but still it is seed rather than fruit.   Its value is in what it promises, and what it fits them to become afterwards. Childhood and youth are the time in which we get the wisdom and the power to be something worthy and useful when men and women.   You would not like to have only the seeds of flowers and fruits.

The first thing said of Christ's childhood is that
HE "INCREASED IN STATURE."

That is what might be said of all persons. He grew
up, as others grow up. He might have come into the
world as a man, if he had pleased. You read in the
Old Testament of a person coming to the Patriarchs
and the Judges, who is sometimes called a "man,"
sometimes "an angel," and sometimes "God" and
"Lord." Many wise people think that he was Jesus
Christ. But if he was, he appeared then only for a
short time, and in a bodily form which he took for the
purpose. And so, if he had liked, he could have taken
such a form for good, instead of being born like others.
But he choose to be a child.

It is God's plan that people shall grow up from being
little babes to be men and women. It has been so ever
since the creation of the world. *Then* God was obliged
to *make things old;* that is, to make them *as if they
had grown up.* Trees, and animals, and Adam himself, were made large and strong, not small and weak.
But since then, all trees have first been plants or seeds;
and all men, even the wisest and greatest, have heen
children at the beginning. The reason is, that God
has his *rules* and *fixed ways* of working, and he does
not go out of his way without a good cause. When
he goes out of his way to do anything, it is called a

miracle, that is, a wonder. But there have not been any miracles for seventeen hundred years.

Jesus Christ, then, grew, became larger and larger in body; and also in mind. He "waxed strong in spirit." What a wonderful thing is *growth* ! Did you ever think of it? It is so unlike anything that men can do. We can *make* things; that is, if we have something to make them out of; though only God can make things *out of nothing*. And we can plant things, and put them into the sun, and water them, and thus help them to grow. But we cannot make *growing things;* nor can we make growing things grow without soil and air and light and heat.

We make things by putting one thing to another, and a third to those two, and so on. It is, with us, *addition*, piece by piece. But God gives what we call *life* to things, and this life causes all the parts of a plant or an animal to get larger and larger at the same time; and this life takes in the virtue which there is in food and air and earth and light, and turns it into nourishment, that is, makes it into more plant and animal. And thus trees grow and people grow. What a wonderful thing it is !

And so it was that Jesus Christ grew. His "stature" became taller, and his power of thinking became greater. How his mother Mary would look at him and watch his ways and words ! She had a thought that

he was not like a common child. There was a great
deal very wonderful about his birth, which made a
deep impression on her mind ; and it is said that " she
kept all these things, and pondered them in her heart."
All parents notice what their children say and do ; and
are very fond of telling people of it, if there is anything at all clever in it, and sometimes they see clever-
ness where no one but a parent could see it. How
much then must Mary have watched the child Jesus ;
how glad she would be to talk to him, and teach him,
and how carefully she would treasure up all in her
mind. I would give a good deal to have an account of
Christ's childhood written by Mary.

Jesus Christ was A VERY GOOD CHILD.

He is called "the *holy* child Jesus." The word
"holy" means *set apart* for God. It is used in the
Old Testament not only of people, but of things, as
days, places, and so on. It does not mean, of course,
that they were religious or moral ; for there must be a
mind and a *will* in order to be religious or moral.
But these things were *set apart* for God's service, and
thus became sacred.

    When *people* are called holy, now, it means that they
are set apart to God's service of *their own accord ;* that
they *like* serving God, that what pleases him pleases

them, that their will is to do what he wills them to do. And this is true of all Christians. One of the names given to them in the New Testament is *"saints,"* which means "holy ones."

Jesus Christ *was always holy.* He was not like us in this respect. There never was anything in him from which sin could come; there was no *root* of sin in him, no *fountain* of sin in him. He was "holy, harmless, undefiled, and separate from sinners." What a sad thought it is, that Jesus Christ was the only child that ever lived of whom it could be said, "In him was no sin." There are a thousand millions of persons living now, and the world is nearly six thousand years old, and yet there never has been one except Jesus who was always holy, and only holy. How it must grieve him who made them all.

We are not holy by nature. We have to *become* holy; but we may become so. Jesus Christ came into the world because he wished us to become so. This is the reason why he was called "Jesus," which is *Saviour*, because he "saves from sin." Christ became a holy man, that men might become holy. And he became a "holy child," that children might become holy. You know that we all like others to be like ourselves, if we are good and kind; and Jesus Christ, being perfectly good, and perfectly kind, wished us to be like him; and he lived and died among us that, as Paul says, we "might be conformed to his image."

What *a blessed thing* it is to be holy! What a beautiful object is a holy child! The *stars* are very beautiful, and the *flowers* are very beautiful, and the *birds* are very beautiful; but a holy child is far, far more beautiful than any of them. Sometimes children have very beautiful *forms* and *faces*, and people love to look at them and say, "What a lovely child that is!" And sometimes children have very beautiful *minds*, such a nice way of thinking, and of saying what they think; aud people like to listen to them. But, oh! there is nothing in the most beautiful body or mind that ever was made at all equal to "the beauties of holiness," to the love and service of God. Angels admire holy children. Jesus Christ loves them.

There is much that is charming in all young things. They are so new, and so fresh. Under the law of Moses the sacrifices were young. And then they may have so much before them in life. Jesus Christ said once, when his Apostles were quarelling, that unless they "became as little children, they could not enter into the kingdom of God." And when children are holy, there is nothing in heaven or earth that is more pleasant or more promising. As Dr. Watts says,

When we devote our youth to God
  'Tis pleasing in his eyes;
A flower, when offered in the bud,
  Is no vain sacrifice.

Jesus "always did the will" of his Father in heaven. Whatever the Father wished him to *do*, he did it. "I must work the works of him that sent me." And whatever the Father wished him to *suffer*, he suffered. Even of the bitter "cup" of Gethsemane, he said, "Not my will, but thine be done." And, therefore, no wonder he was God's "chosen, in whom his soul delighted."

But Jesus grew in favour with *men*. There must have been much about him they could not understand, and something they did not like ; but they approved him. Even bad people have a conscience, something in them which tells them what is right, and likes to see it done by others. A great deal of what bad people say against good people is only to try to put down their own consciences—to dare and drown their own consciences.

When Dr. Doddridge's little daughter, a very good and kind child, was asked, "Why everybody loved her ?" she said, "I do not know, unless it is because I love everybody." That was reason enough. Jesus loved everybody, as a child ; and everybody loved him. And this is our best way to be loved also.

THE CHILDHOOD OF JESUS CHRIST.

All living things are small at first ;
  For God who made them all,
And could as well have made them great,
  Preferred to make them small.

The largest trees from cuttings rise,
  The oak from acorn springs,
And animals of largest size
  Were first but little things.

And man, of all God's works on earth
  The chiefest, king and priest,
Is but a tiny babe at birth,
  In many things the least.

The Lord of glory, like the rest
  Of men, his course began ;
Was first an infant at the breast,
  And grew to be a man.

And well he grew, in form and face,
  And better still in soul,
While wisdom gave him strength and grace,
  And favour crowned the whole.

O may I grow as Jesus grew,
  Alike in mind and size ;
And, learning more of what he knew,
  Be holy and be wise !

CHAPTER IV

THE CHILD JESUS IN THE TEMPLE, AND AT HOME.

Luke ii. 48—51.—"AND WHEN THEY SAW HIM, THEY WERE AMAZED : AND HIS MOTHER SAID UNTO HIM, SON, WHY HAST THOU THUS DEALT WITH US? BEHOLD, THY FATHER AND I HAVE SOUGHT THEE SORROWING. AND HE SAID UNTO THEM, HOW IS IT THAT YE SOUGHT ME? WIST YE NOT THAT I MUST BE ABOUT MY FATHER'S BUSINESS? AND THEY UNDERSTOOD NOT THE SAYING WHICH HE SPAKE UNTO THEM. AND HE WENT DOWN WITH THEM, AND CAME TO NAZARETH, AND WAS SUBJECT UNTO THEM ; BUT HIS MOTHER KEPT ALL THESE SAYINGS IN HER HEART."

THIS is the only passage that tells of any of Christ's words or actions until he entered on his public work, when thirty years of age. But it is a passage full of interest. It gives us *two views* of Jesus Christ, each of which should please and teach us by itself, but more so when looked at along with the other.

Look at the child Jesus IN THE TEMPLE.

The Jewish temple was a very fine building in Jerusalem, set apart to the service of God. God was the king of the Jews. Jerusalem was "the city of

the great king." The temple was his palace. He is
said to have dwelt there. And there he received the
sacrifices and offerings of his subjects. .

The Jewish law required all males of twenty years
of age to appear three times a year before God in
Jerusalem. The times were the feast of the Passover,
the feast of Pentecost, and the feast of Tabernacles.
It was the custom for children, when they had reached
their twelfth year, to go also ; for then they were
called "sons of the law," and were expected from that
time to keep the law. Women were not commanded
to observe these feasts, but they might if they liked ;
and no doubt many of the more zealous of them did so.

It was now the feast of the Passover, which lasted
seven days ; and Joseph, with Mary his wife, visited
Jerusalem, to keep the feast. Jesus, being twelve
years of age, went with them. Having " fulfilled the
days," Joseph and Mary returned homewards in one
of those companies in which Jewish pilgrims travelled
for society and safety. Being used to the wisdom and
goodness of their child, they had perfect trust in him,
and therefore went their way, taking it for granted
that he was in the company, although he had really
stayed behind in Jerusalem. After three days, they
found him in the temple. What had he been doing
there ?

He had been sitting in the midst of the doctors,

D

listening to them, and asking them questions. And
the people wondered at the knowledge and quickness
that he showed.

When you read of the Jewish temple, you must not
think of a church or a chapel among ourselves ; for it
was a very different kind of place. There was not
only the part which was used for the worship of God,
consisting of courts for the priests and the people, and
the Holy of Holies, where was the mercy-seat, " the
throne of grace," over which was the Shekinah, the
sign of God's presence ; but round these there were a
great number of rooms and halls. Many people lived
in the chambers, who had to do different things in
connection with the temple. And here, among other
things, learned men taught the young people.

Now it was in one of these schools that Jesus was.
He was not preaching, as he is sometimes supposed to
have been. He was not asking questions with a view
to puzzle the doctors. He was hearing what they said,
earning of them, and making inquiries, as Jewish
scholars might do, in order to get more knowledge.
So that there was nothing rude or forward, or at all
out of the common way, in what Jesus did.

His parents found him after a long and anxious
search. It is a terrible thing for parents to lose a
child ; for one dearly loved, and not able to take care
of himself, to be gone, they know not where ; to meet

with they know not what; and fall into the hands of they know not whom. Oh ! this is heart-breaking. Children should never, if they can help it, cause this great trouble to those who love them. Children should always think that, though *they* know where they are, their parents may not ; and they should never go anywhere without their parents' knowledge and consent.

Mary somewhat scolded Jesus for his absence. "Son, why hast thou thus dealt with us ? Behold, thy father and I have sought thee sorrowing. And he said unto them, How is it that ye sought me ? Wist ye not that I must be about my Father's business ? And they understood not the saying which he spake unto them." It is clear that they might have understood it ; or at least better than they did. There had been many things since his birth, strange things, things that do not happen to other children, and Mary had "kept them and pondered them in her heart." There had been much to show that Jesus was not a common child, and that he was born for no common purpose ; that God had a great work for him to do.

Now what may we learn from Christ's first visit to the temple ? and from what he did there ? and from the words he spake to his mother ? What do we see in the child Jesus at the age of twelve ?

We have a child raised up by God for a glorious end, sent into the world as a messenger, a martyr, a mediator; that he might teach, and live for, and die for, man. We have this child being prepared by the spirit of wisdom, and knowledge of God's word and law, for his great and lonely work. We have this child conscious of his high destiny, looking forward to it, yearning after it. We have him quite at home with the thoughts of it, and quite at home with what belonged to it. Great men, who have been only men, have often had, when young, a strong feeling that they were meant and made for some noble task. Great men still living, or not long dead, have believed that they would become noted, before there was any outward sign of it. Samson, the strong deliverer of his people, when a "child, grew, and the Lord blessed him; and the Spirit of the Lord began to move him at times." And Jesus Christ, when only twelve years old, knew that he was set apart as God's Son for God's service; looked upon the temple as his Father's house; astonished even the doctors of the law by the amount of his knowledge, and the ripeness of his judgment; and longed to be engaged in his Father's work.

Look at the child Jesus AT HOME.

"And he went down with them, and came to Nazareth, and was subject unto them." He had been subject unto them *before* this time, or they would not have

been a day without knowing where he was. The fact
that they had left him at Jerusalem while thinking
that he was in the company, showed that they could
trust him, that they had had no trouble with him. It
is a grand thing when a child can be trusted, when so
young a child as he was can be trusted. It is a grand
thing when so much thought and care and regard for
others' feelings are joined to childish years.

He was "*subject unto them,*" as all children ought
to be subject unto their parents. It is the will of God
it should be so. It is necessary. If disobedience to
parents could be allowed, the world would soon be in
confusion and ruin. It would be like ignorance teaching knowledge, and weakness governing strength. We
depend on our parents as much for guidance as for
food and clothing. No wonder that God has always
been very jealous for the honour of parents, who are
in his place, and have to act for him in a special way.
No wonder that Paul says, "Children, obey your
parents in the Lord" (that is, in Christ) : "for this is
right. Honour thy father and mother, (which is the
first commandment with promise ;) that it may be well
with thee, and thou mayest live long on the earth."—
Eph. vi. 1—3.

But what I wish you to notice, now, is that *Jesus
Christ* was subject unto his parents. If he was, how
much more should we be ? He was God's Son in a

way no one else ever was, and he knew it. The temple
was his home in a sense true of no one else, and he
felt it. He had before him a work never given to any
one else to do, and he longed for it. And yet, like any
other child, he honoured his earthly parents, obeyed
them, acknowledged their rule, and followed their in-
structions.

He was *above* them, yet he submitted to them.
Children often set their parents at nought, because
they think themselves above them. Perhaps they are
clever, and their parents are dull and slow in their
minds. Perhaps they have had a good education, and
their parents have had but little schooling. Perhaps
they have been taught how to behave in good society,
and their parents are rude and awkward in their man-
ners. Perhaps they have reason to expect much of
this world's wealth, and their parents are very poor.
And, *therefore*, they do not "honour" their parents,
but slight them. They do not obey them. They perhaps scarcely treat them with civility. They may
even turn them into ridicule, and laugh at their words
and ways. If any children who read this book act in
this way, let me beseech them to think of Jesus Christ.
He was far more above his parents than any of you can
be above yours. He had a divine nature, and a divine
work. And yet he was "subject unto them," because
they were his parents; and in that respect had a right
to be obeyed.

You have seen that not only was he above them, but he was above them because he was *a child of God* in a particular sense ; and he had to do *a work for God* which he alone could do. And yet he obeyed them. Sometimes children are tempted to despise or neglect their parents because they feel that they are above them in *religious things.* In plain language, *they are Christians, and their parents are not.* Perhaps their parents do not believe the Bible. Perhaps they neglect it. Perhaps they live in sin. This is a serious snare. When a child who loves Jesus has parents who do not care for him, and perhaps hate him ; it is very hard for that child to pay proper respect to those parents. And yet even then we must make a difference between the *office* of parent and the *person* who holds it. We may honour the *father* when we cannot honour the *man* who is our father. We may honour the *mother*, when we cannot honour the *woman* who is our mother. God has not told us to love or reverence what is wrong or foolish in either father or mother. He has told us to respect and observe *the place* which he has given them in connection with us. The *king* or the *master* may be bad *men*, but they are to be obeyed.

Once more. We may learn *not to despise any one or any thing,* however poor and mean in our opinion. Jesus Christ washed his disciples' feet, and he said to them, "If I, then, your Lord and Master, have washed your feet; ye also ought to wash one another's feet." He was in the "form of God," and he took the form of a man, a suffering and mortal man, and Paul says, "Let this mind be in you which was also in Christ Jesus."

We are to "condescend to men of low estate;" and to things of small importance. It is not a proof of a great mind to scorn or neglect what is little. Some people seem to think so, but they are not great people. They are small people. God thinks nothing too small for *him* to notice and take care of. He "makes small the drops of rain." "Not a sparrow falleth to the ground without our Father." How much less does it become *us* to think that we are above minding small things?

My dear children. It is not *what* we do, but HOW we do it, that is the great matter. A good painter will make a little picture worth more than a bad painter will make a large picture worth. The question is, not what is our *lot* in the world, but what is our *life?* Are we living in a *holy* way, so as to please God? If so, we are "great in *his* sight;" greater than bad men, though they are very rich, and though they have a great deal of power.

THE CHILD JESUS IN THE TEMPLE
AND AT HOME.

Upon that sacred spot
His childhood felt at home,
It was his Heavenly Father's house
To which his heart had come.
And in his Father's law he found
A better home than holy ground.

He had, though child was he,
A learning deep and true ;
He knew how great he was to be, '
And felt as if he knew ;
And with his young yet manly soul
Divinely yearned to reach the goal.

And yet he did not spurn
The lesser human ties,
Nor from his Heavenly Parent learn
His human to despise ;
But rather let his glory shine
To make his earthly lot divine.

Lord, may thy childhood bring
This lesson to my breast ;
May I revere each meaner thing
In honour of the best ;
Nor, for the sake of good in store,
Regard the present less, but more !

CHAPTER V

CHRIST'S SERMON ON A CHILD.

Matt. xviii. 2.—" AND JESUS CALLED A LITTLE CHILD UNTO HIM, AND SET HIM IN THE MIDST OF THEM."

THE Lord Jesus Christ had been upon the mount with three of his Apostles, Peter, James, and John; and while praying there, his body had become very glorious, his face had shone like the sun, and his raiment had been white as the light. There had come a bright cloud, the sign of God's presence. Moses and Elijah had talked with Jesus about his coming death. And a voice had said, " This is my beloved Son, in whom I am well pleased; hear ye him." All this was intended to prepare Jesus, and his disciples, for the trials and sorrows that were before them.

But it is very likely that at first it had a bad effect on some of them; for on the way, the Apostles fell into a warm dispute about who should be greatest in Christ's kingdom; that is, the kingdom which they thought he was going to set up in the world. The fact that three of them had been chosen to see Christ in his glory perhaps made some or all of the others envious, and they quarrelled about it.

You may learn from this that good people may have much in them that is not good, and may turn what is good to evil. And you may learn also what bad things pride and ambition are. Paul once went to heaven, and was in danger of being puffed up by it. Those disciples, who ought to have felt like a family, are giving way to bad tempers and passions. What was done on the mount, which should have made them all glad and solemn, leads to quarrelling. And those who should have been pleased that their brethren saw such a sight, are jealous and angry.

Well, Jesus Christ preached a short sermon to them, in order to set them right, and he took a text; but not, as ministers take texts now, out of the Bible. His text was *a little child*, a very strange but very nice text. And he preached such a beautiful sermon on that text, which I should have liked to hear, and I dare say that you would too. For even those who were sent, at one time, to take him up, came back without him to their cruel masters, saying, "Never man spake like this man." How delightful it must have been to hear him speak about little children! What did he say?

Jesus Christ taught that ALL HIS DISCIPLES MUST BECOME LIKE LITTLE CHILDREN.

"Verily I say unto you, Except ye be converted, and become as little children, ye shall not enter into the kingdom of heaven."

Now, you must think a little, that you may see just what Jesus Christ meant. I can fancy a child getting a very wrong notion of his meaning. You must not suppose that children are all good, and that people must become like them in all respects.

This child was a *little* one. It was so small that Mark says Jesus took him into his arms. It was, therefore, most likely younger than any child who can read and understand what I am now saying.

There is much that is innocent and pleasant in little children, *which they cannot be praised for.* They do not know that it is good. It is with them as it is with young animals. *They* are often very nice—young lambs, young kittens, and other things; but they cannot be called *good* as men can be called good, because they have not the knowledge and the will that men have. So little children are not old enough to be good of their own accord.

What Christ meant was this. Little children are generally humble, meek, and modest. "Whosoever shall *humble* himself as this little child," are Christ's words. And Christ was speaking against pride, passion, and envy. So David said, "Lord, my heart is not haughty, nor mine eyes lofty : neither do I exercise myself in great matters, or in things too high for me. Surely I have behaved and quieted myself, as a child that is weaned of his mother : my soul is even as a weaned child." Little children are simple, without guile, and do not put on airs. They conceal nothing ; pretend to nothing ; and, if they are hurt or offended, it passes away like a summer's cloud, and the sun of love and joy shines again. They believe what they are told, for they have not lost faith through being deceived. A king's child, if let, would play with a beggar's child. And their wants and wishes are very small and few.

Now Christ says we must be like children *in these things. We must believe what God says*, as little children. They take things just as they are. They never think of doubting the word of a parent. They believe everything is as it seems to be ; and because a rainbow *looks as if* it was near, they will run after it, and try to catch it. Now we must believe what God says in this way. When we are quite sure that he speaks to us, we must take him at his word. Men are very angry when they are thought to speak falsely ; and John says, " He that believeth not God hath made him a liar." No wonder that a man who makes God a liar cannot be saved.

There are many things which God says that we cannot understand. A child cannot see the meaning or the reasons of everything that his father or mother says; but it is told that when it is older it perhaps will. So now we must believe all that God says, just because he says it, and he knows far more than we do: and perhaps, as Christ told Peter, "What we know not now, we shall know hereafter."

Again, *we must receive what God gives us*, as little children. The Apostles disputed as to who should be greatest in the kingdom which they expected Jesus was about to set up. That is, they quarrelled who should have most honour, most power, most money; just as children often quarrel about the nicest toy or largest cake. And they had to become little children, so as to be content with whatever was given them. How small a thing will please a very young child. A little sweetmeat, or simple play, will make it chuckle and crow with delight. And so we must be "content with such things as we have," and "in everything give thanks."

We often go wrong here. We don't like taking God's gifts, *as gifts*. We want to be able to c'aim them, as if we deserved them. Many people will not have God's grace because they are too proud. They can't bear the thought of being beggars, even to *him*. They want to *do* something to be rewarded. They

won't owe God a debt. And we cannot be saved at
all in this way. Salvation *must* be a gift. "The gift
of God is eternal life." And we must all learn to say,
"Thanks be unto God for his unspeakable gift."

And then we often are not *satisfied with what God
gives us.* We think we have less than we ought, like
the labourers in the parable, who complained that,
after working many hours, they received no more than
those who had worked but one hour. We quarrel
with our lot in life, our business, the troubles that
come upon us, the sickness and pain of the body, and
"forget the exhortation that speaketh unto us as unto
sons, My son, despise not thou the chastening of the
Lord, nor faint when thou art rebuked of him, for
whom the Lord loveth he chasteneth, and scourgeth
every son whom he receiveth."

And the same spirit of childhood will be seen in
doing what God bids us. A father's commands are
not like a master's. They are kinder in themselves,
and in the feeling from which they come. "This is
the love of God, that we keep his commandments, and
his commandments are not grievous." Whenever God
calls us, the answer of the child Samuel should be
ours, ' Speak, Lord, for thy servant heareth." It is
not for us to dictate to God, to question his orders, or
to resist them. Our business is *obedience.* "I made
haste and delayed not to keep thy commandments."

And Christ says *that the more we have of this child-
like spirit, the more he thinks of us.*   "Whosoever
shall humble himself as this little child, the same shall
be greatest in the kingdom of heaven."   What a
strange kingdom it is ! The world praises and honours
the proud, the warlike, the ambitious, the rich.   But
Jesus says, " Blessed are the poor in spirit, for theirs
is the kingdom of heaven."   " Blessed are the meek,
for they shall inherit the earth."   " Blessed are the
peacemakers, for they shall be called the children of
God."   " If any man will be great among you, let
him be your servant." .

JESUS CHRIST THINKS A GREAT DEAL OF THOSE
WHO ARE LIKE LITTLE CHILDREN ; AND OF THE WAY
IN WHICH THE WORLD TREATS THEM.

" Whoso shall receive one such little child in my
name receiveth me."   That means, out of regard to
Christ, and because he is a child of God, and has
Christ's spirit in him.   What a thing to say !   We
should all receive Christ if he came among us.   We
should feel ourselves honoured by his coming under
our roof.   We should give him the best of all that we
possessed.   And yet Christ teaches us that if we
welcome and honour a child-like Christian, we honour
him.

And this was not the only time that Jesus spoke in this way. The twenty-fifth chapter of Matthew's Gospel contains one of Christ's discourses, in which there is the longest account we have anywhere of the day of judgment ; and he divides men into two classes, those who "go away into everlasting punishment," and those who go away "into everlasting life." And why is this difference, this great and endless difference? Jesus describes himself as having been hungry and thirsty, and naked and sick, and a stranger and a prisoner. And he says that when so, some men were kind to him, and some neglected him. And when the righteous ask when they were kind to him, and when the wicked ask when they neglected him, he says that what was done to his "brethren" was done to him, and what was not done to his brethren was not done to him.

What a dreadful word he has for those who offend these children of grace! "Whoso shall offend one of these little ones which believe in me, it were better for him that a millstone were hanged about his neck, and that he were drowned in the depth of the sea." Better *that*, better an *awful death* !

Oh! take care how you treat Christians! Even children sometimes mock them, and call them names, and say and think bad things of them   If ever you feel inclined to do so, remember what Jesus Christ has

E

said.   They are *his*.   He loves them.   He feels himself honoured when they are honoured, and injured
when they are injured.   "He that toucheth you
toucheth the apple of mine eye."

JESUS CHRIST SAYS TWO THINGS ABOUT THOSE WHO
ARE LIKE CHILDREN.

He says that *they are saved*.   And he says that
they have good angels to take care of them.
He says that "it is not the will of your Father
which is in heaven that one of these little ones should
perish ;" and also that "the Son of man is come to
save that which was lost."   And then he goes on to say
that if a man has a hundred sheep, and one of them
goes astray, he leaves them all to seek that one, and if
he finds it, he has more joy in it than in all the rest
that have not been lost at all.   You have felt that
yourselves.   We all feel it.   When we find anything
we have lost, it makes us more glad at the time than
the thought of many greater things that have not been
lost.   It is joy after sorrow, and joy instead of sorrow.
And so the good shepherd rejoices when he finds those
who have wandered from his fold, whether sheep or
lambs.
We need saving in this way.   The youngest who
know right from wrong need it.   "We all like sheep

have gone astray," and must "return to the shepherd and bishop of souls," the pastor and overlooker of souls. That is *salvation*, the being found by Jesus, and brought back to his fold. It means being made good, and happy in God's love. And all God's little ones are saved thus.

Christ says further, "Take heed that ye despise not one of these little ones; for I say unto you, That in heaven their angels do always behold the face of my Father which is in heaven." You have heard of "guardian angels." There are many pretty little songs about them, how they watch over people when they are not thinking of them, and keep away what would hurt them. Dr. Watts has this verse,—

> I lay my body down to sleep,
>   Peace is the pillow for my head,
> While well appointed angels keep
>   Their watchful stations round my bed.

The Jews believed in guardian angels. When Peter was released by an angel from prison, and stood at the door of Mary's house, the disciples within would not believe that it was Peter, but said, "It is his angel." Paul says, "Are they not all ministering spirits, sent forth to minister for them who shall be heirs of salvation?"

God does as much as he can by means of others. He could do, if he liked, without his creatures

altogether. He has to make them, to give them all
their powers, and to keep them day after day. He has
to guide and to strengthen them in their work. He has
to bless what they do and make it answer his ends.
So God does not depend on any of his creatures ; but
they all depend on him. The greatest depend on him
as much as the least. I might say *more;* because,
being the greatest, they have more that needs to be
preserved by him. But yet God uses his creatures to
do his will.

It is for *their sakes* that he uses them, not his
own. A kind parent will often *make* something for his
child to do, and the child feels glad in being employed. The parent does not *want* his child's help.
He perhaps does not want anything done at all : or he
could do what he wants better himself than his child
could do it. But the child says, " Papa, will you give
me something to do ?" or, " Can you send me on an
errand ?" And the father, to please his child, sets him
a task, or gives him a message. And God, who could
do all things by himself, and with a word, is pleased
to use our little services. *It is good for us.* It is a
pleasure to be employed. It is a way of improving
and bettering ourselves. And by doing good to others,
they become more dear and loving to us.

Jesus says that God employs "angels" to take care
of us. He does not need angels to do it. But angels,

like men, must have something to do; and they are
very fond of doing good. They sang and praised God
when Jesus, the Saviour of men, was born; and they
rejoice when one poor sinner repents, and, like a lost
sheep, is brought back into the fold of the good shepherd. And to serve Jesus, and help to save sinners,
is their greatest delight.

All who have a child-like spirit—all who receive the
kingdom of God simply, meekly, and with joy, have
angels to guard them. What an honour! To be
watched over by spirits, holy spirits, who "excell in
strength," and live in the presence of God! What
an honour to have angels for servants, for companions,
for guards! The kings and great men of the world
have no such honour. They may have servants in
livery, and soldiers in arms, and attendants in lace
and gold, to wait upon them; but Christians have
angels. Little children, if like Jesus, have angels to
take care of them! And angels are not angry or
sorry at having to do it, but are very happy that
they have the task, and would not give it up on any
account.

And if angels are thus employed for Christians,
nothing else that they want will be withheld from
them. If angels help and defend and guide us now,
what must God have in store for us in heaven!

"The angel of the Lord encampeth round about

them that fear him, and delivereth them. O taste and see that the Lord is good : blessed is the man that trusteth in him.   The young lions do lack, and suffer hunger ; but they that seek the Lord shall not want any good thing.   Come, ye children, hearken unto me; I will teach you the fear of the Lord."—Psal. xxxiv. 7—11.

A PRAYER TO BE MADE CHILD-LIKE.

Blest Saviour, let me be a child,
   A little child of thine ;
Thou hast on infant-spirits smiled,
   O kindly smile on mine.

Make me a child in simple ways,
   In heart more simple still ;
Believing all the Father says,
   And doing all his will.

Give me a nature pure and true,
   My evil one control ;
And day by day thy grace renew
   The childhood of my soul.

May this sweet spirit ne'er depart,
   Midst all my joys and cares ;
And may I be a child in heart,
   Although a man in years.

CHAPTER VI.

CHRIST'S WELCOME TO CHILDREN.

Mark x. 13—16.—"AND THEY BROUGHT YOUNG CHILDREN TO HIM, THAT
HE SHOULD TOUCH THEM: AND HIS DISCIPLES REBUKED THOSE THAT
BROUGHT THEM. BUT WHEN JESUS SAW IT HE WAS MUCH DISPLEASED,
AND SAID UNTO THEM, SUFFER THE LITTLE CHILDREN TO COME UNTO
ME, AND FORBID THEM NOT: FOR OF SUCH IS THE KINGDOM OF GOD.
VERILY I SAY UNTO YOU, WHOSOVER SHALL NOT RECEIVE THE KING-
DOM OF GOD AS A LITTLE CHILD, HE SHALL NOT ENTER THEREIN.
AND HE TOOK THEM UP IN HIS ARMS, PUT HIS HANDS UPON THEM,
AND BLESSED THEM."

THESE words are some of the most beautiful words
in all the Bible, and children especially should love
them. They show how Jesus Christ felt about children, when he was on earth ; and they also show how
he feels about them now that he is in heaven.

Many people don't love children. There are parents
who don't love their own children. We read in the
Bible that even mothers may forget their little ones,
though it is mentioned as a strange and shocking thing.
But the people who don't love children are generally
those who have none of their own. Some think
themselves *too great* to care for children. But they

are not so great as Jesus Christ. And yet the prophet Isaiah said of him, "Behold, the Lord God will come with strong hand, and his arm shall rule for him : behold, his reward is with him, and his work before him. He shall feed his flock like a shepherd : he shall gather the lambs in his arm, and carry them in his bosom, and shall gently lead those that are with young." What a mixture of greatness and gentleness, of power and love !

CHILDREN ARE BROUGHT TO CHRIST.

Infants and young children, some of them in arms, are brought to Jesus. We are not told by whom ; but it is most likely by their parents, or other near relatives.

It is not said what they thought of Jesus. Perhaps they had not very clear thoughts about him. It is certain they had not such thoughts as we may have ; for so much was not known of Jesus then as is known now, and these people did not know all that could have been known then.

They knew, at least, that Christ was no common man. When great men are in a place, men who have made a noise in the world, people are very anxious to see them, and if they can get to speak to them, or to shake hands with them, they are much set up. You have read of Zacchæus, who wished to see Jesus, of whom he had heard, and, as he was a short man, and the crowd blocked the view, ran up into a sycamore tree.—Luke xix. 1—4. And now, when a great man, a great soldier, or a great statesman, or a queen, or a prince, comes into a district, how large a multitude gathers together, and windows are filled, and people get on to the roofs of houses, and walls, and lamp-posts, to catch a peep. And this is done just for a moment's look, and to be able to say afterwards that they had seen the great person. And, at such times, people will drag their children through a crowd, and lift them up in their arms, and put them on their shoulders, that they also may have to say that they had seen the great person. And if by any chance the great person should notice or speak to them, or their children, they never forget it all the days of their lives.

These people felt in this way. They knew that Jesus was a wonderful man, and a wonderfully good man; and they wished their little ones to be noticed and "touched" by him. But they did more. For Matthew says they wanted Jesus "to put his hands on the children and pray." It was not therefore a foolish fondness, or a silly faith, but a true love and piety that moved them. They had a high opinion of Jesus as a man of God, and believed that his solemn prayer and blessing would be worth having for their little ones; and they were right.

And, my dear children, there is nothing in this world that those who love you wisely would sooner do for you than bring you to Jesus. It is a blessed thing that Jesus is still within reach of us. We cannot see him nor hear him, for he left the world long ago, and the body he has is in heaven. But he can see and hear us. When he was going away, he said to his disciples, "Lo, I am with you always, even to the end of the world." And he did not mean just those few that he spoke to then, but all who should be his disciples, that is, all who should learn of him and obey him for ever. Stephen saw him and prayed to him. Paul prayed to him. And all Christians are said to "call on the name of the Lord Jesus Christ." *You* may do this. You may be brought to Jesus by those who love you, in their prayers. And you may come to Jesus yourselves in prayer.

I said that all those who love you *wisely* will wish to bring you to Jesus. Your parents and other persons may love you much, and yet not wish to bring you to Jesus; but that is, because *they don't know Jesus themselves :* they don't know how great and good he is, and how much he can do for those that he loves and blesses. But if your parents really know him and love him, they would rather you came to Jesus than that anything else happened to you. They would rather you came to Jesus than that you were taken to the Queen of England, and brought up by her, and loaded with all the favours that she could give you. They would rather that you had the blessing of Jesus than that you had all the money and all the honour and all the power in the world.

You can come to Jesus yourselves. You are old enough. You know enough. You can pray. You can say, "O Lord, convert my soul, for Jesus Christ's sake." That short prayer a good minister made a young person promise to say every day until he saw her again. And it pleased God to hear it. She thought upon that prayer, and why he asked her to say it ; and thinking of it made her feel ; and then she prayed it *in earnest,* and God answered it ; and when she met the minister again she had to thank him with a joyful heart for making her promise to say that short prayer. Will you pray it ?

THE DISCIPLES SCOLD THOSE WHO BROUGHT THESE CHILDREN TO JESUS CHRIST.

They perhaps thought it a very useless thing, as the children were too young to understand what Jesus might do or say to them. They perhaps thought it a piece of folly or vanity ; for parents are often smiled at or scolded for the fuss they make about their little ones, as if other people could think as much of them, and care as much for them, as they do themselves. And perhaps they thought that Jesus Christ was too great a person to be troubled in this way, and that little children were beneath his notice. I dare say they had no children of their own, and so could not enter into the feelings of parents.

But how strange it is that *the apostles* should rebuke these parents, and try to stop them ! The apostles were Christ's special friends and followers. He had chosen them on purpose to preach his Gospel, and bring people to him to be saved. And yet they try to prevent children coming to him! And in other cases they did the same. They tried to stop people who wished to be cured, or who wished to have those near and dear to them cured, by him.

It is very odd and sad to think of. But then we must remember that the apostles *did not understand Jesus Christ now,* nor till after he had left the world. Though they were men in age and size, they were children in knowledge. They thought that Christ came into the world to be a king, like any other king ; to give good places to his friends, and to destroy his enemies. They did not know that he came to save men's souls, that he loved all men and all children, and was never so glad as when he could do them good. They learnt better afterwards, when the Holy Spirit was given to them on the day of Pentecost. Then, their minds were filled with light, and their hearts with love; and they would not have prevented parents bringing their little ones to Jesus after that.

There are people, now, who would prevent children coming to Jesus, if they could; and many who do. There are many who don't think anything of him, and don't care about him. They don't love him themselves, and don't wish others to love him. Many persons have very foolish notions of religion, and think it a dull and sorrowful thing, although it is a bright and pleasant one; and therefore they would have it put off until old age or sickness comes, and nothing else can be attended to.

But even "*disciples*" may hinder children coming to Jesus. For true Christians are not always wise; and some are very foolish, have very silly thoughts, and very silly ways of speaking their thoughts. And some are cold and harsh in their manner, and have bad tempers, and are not at all the kind of persons to win the hearts of the young, or to help them in good things. And some are so different from what they ought to be in conduct and disposition, that they set children against religion altogether. I have read of a child who, when told that an aunt would go to heaven, said, "Then I don't want to go."

But do not forget this. If you can understand what you are reading now, you are old enough *to come to Christ for yourselves;* and you have no right *to let anyone prevent you coming.* And no one can keep you away if you are willing to come. We read in the Gospels of people who pressed forward that they might "touch the hem of Christ's garment, and be made whole." And whoever and whatever comes between your souls and Jesus Christ, you must not regard; but make up your minds to obtain his grace and blessing. You must be like the person who once said, "If only two are saved, I will be one of them!"

JESUS CHRIST WELCOMES THE CHILDREN.

And here there are three things to be considered. What Christ *felt.* What Christ *said.* And what Christ *did.*

What Christ *felt.* He was "much displeased." It is not always wrong to be angry. We should always be angry with what is *wrong.* Jesus Christ was very angry with bad people, but it was with a holy anger. It was calm and grave, not passionate and revengeful. "He was angry, being grieved for the hardness of their hearts." Once, some of the apostles wished that a Samaritan village might be destroyed, because the. people would not receive him; but he answered them, "Ye know not what manner of spirit ye are of; for the Son of man is not come to destroy men's lives but to save them." Jesus Christ could hate men's conduct, and yet love their souls.

There were many things that displeased Jesus here. The apostles ought to have felt differently themselves towards the children. And they ought to have known him better than to think they were pleasing him by what they did. They had been with him long enough to know what kind of heart he had. And it was but a short time ago that he had taken a child, and put him in the midst of them, and said that they must become like one, or they could not be his disciples. They were, therefore, to blame for what they did; and Jesus might well be angry with them.

And he is angry with all those who keep children from him. He does not come forward to reprove them, and they cannot see a cloud upon his face, and hear the severe tones of his voice. But he knows all they say and do, and remembers it; and he will punish them for it some day, unless they change their minds, and become more like him.

What Christ *said.* "Suffer little children to come unto me, and forbid them not: for of such is the kingdom of God." Precious words! If he had only said, "Let them come," it would have been much; but it would not have gone further than *those* children; and it would not have been certain that the *souls* of children were included in Christ's favour. But when he added, "Of such is the kingdom of God," we are sure that he meant more children than those, and meant a greater blessing than any earthly good."

"The kingdom of God," and "the kingdom of heaven," mean much the same as the Church and Gospel of Jesus Christ. God is a king over all. Angels and men and animals and things without life are all his servants; and whether they know it or not, and whether they wish it or not, they all are made to work out his plans. But he has another kingdom, a kingdom of truth and grace and love. This kingdom is in men's souls. And only they are its subjects who "obey the will of God from the heart." In this kingdom, God is a loving Father, and his subjects are sons and daughters, and his laws are laws of liberty and love. Now Christ says that this kingdom belongs to little children.

It belongs to them before they are old enough to know it. It belongs to them as soon as they are born. If they die in infancy, they go to heaven, to the kingdom of glory above, to be for ever with Jesus Christ. And if they live on earth, this kingdom is theirs until they refuse it, and put it away from them by unbelief and sin. And if children do put the kingdom of God away, they may seek it again. If, after they are old enough to answer for themselves, they should turn their backs on Jesus, they may still become members

F

of his kingdom; and he will welcome them more warmly than those who have lived many years without his grace.

What Christ *did.* "He took them up in his arms, put his hands upon them, and blessed them." How ashamed the apostles must have been, after their rough words! And how delighted the parents must have been, after being so blamed! In all ages, people have valued the blessing of those who were very good. How much more must the blessing of Jesus have been worth! You remember how often the apostle Paul, in his Epistles, wishes this blessing for his readers. "The grace of our Lord Jesus Christ be with you all." "The Lord Jesus Christ be with thy spirit." It includes everything, salvation here and hereafter. May it be ours!

Would you not like to know what became of these children? Their parents would tell them, as they grew up, what Jesus had done to them, and said about them. Some of them would, perhaps, become Christians. Indeed, an ancient writer says that one of them became afterwards the famous Ignatius, who was, for forty years, the bishop of Antioch; and was thrown among wild beasts at Rome, and devoured by them, because he was a Christian!

But be that as it may, one thing is certain, that if you come to Jesus in the right way while young, you

will grow up to be true Christians; and will be able
to learn more of him, and do more for him, than those
who put off coming to him till they are grown up.
There is nothing like beginning early with anything
good.   Plants are trained young.   Animals are broken
in young.   And the proper time to give the heart to
Jesus Christ is when it is tender and fresh ; and
before it gets very bad, and is made hard by sin.

CHRIST'S WELCOME TO CHILDREN.

It was not strange that parents brought
  Their little children to the Lord,
If they had seen the works he wrought,
  And listened to his loving word.

But it was strange that those who trod
  His path, and heard him, day by day,
Should think they pleased the Son of God
  By keeping little ones away.

They knew not that he took the place
  And form of child for children's sake,
And that the blessings of his grace
  The child-like heart alone can take.

Fain would I come.   May Christ receive
  And bless me, as he only can,
And, spite of all my evil, give
  The boon so great for child and man !

Young lambs were brought to God and slain
  Of old by sacrificial knife ;
I bring myself, O Christ, to gain
  From thee a new and nobler life.

CHAPTER VII

CHRIST GIVING LIFE AND HEALTH TO CHILDREN.

John iv. 50.—"JESUS SAITH UNTO HIM, GO THY WAY, THY SON LIVETH."

Mark v. 41, 42.—"AND HE TOOK THE DAMSEL BY THE HAND, AND SAID UNTO HER, TALITHA CUMI; WHICH IS, BEING INTERPRETED, DAMSEL, I SAY UNTO THEE, ARISE. AND STRAIGHTWAY THE DAMSEL AROSE AND WALKED; FOR SHE WAS OF THE AGE OF TWELVE YEARS."

Matthew xv. 28.—"THEN JESUS ANSWERED AND SAID UNTO HER, O WOMAN, GREAT IS THY FAITH: BE IT UNTO THEE EVEN AS THOU WILT. AND HER DAUGHTER WAS MADE WHOLE FROM THAT VERY HOUR."

Luke ix. 42.—"AND JESUS REBUKED THE UNCLEAN SPIRIT, AND HEALED THE CHILD, AND DELIVERED HIM AGAIN TO HIS FATHER."

THESE passages are parts of four very beautiful stories, and are taken out of the four Gospels, one out of each Gospel. One of them is in only one Gospel; one of them is in two; and two of them are in three. I hope you will look out all the places, and read them carefully, and compare the different accounts of the same things together. If you do so, you will be much pleased. You will have a delightful view of the love and power which Jesus showed in connection with children.

This is the reason why I have chosen these nice stories to speak to you about. They tell us of the miracles which Jesus Christ did for children ; that is, the cures he made for them, and which no man, however clever, or however powerful, could have made. And as we read them, we may see what Jesus Christ is able and willing to do for children to-day. I do not mean to say that he does *exactly the same things* now ; but he is *as kind and as strong* as when he did them ; and he does other things which are quite as great and good, and things much greater and better. It is very pleasant to think that so many of Christ's most wonderful works were done for the sake of sick and suffering little ones. And it is still more pleasant to think that Jesus Christ, although in heaven, is as much their friend and helper as he was on earth.

CHILDREN MAY SUFFER SORELY IN THIS WORLD.

All these four were children. Some of them are called "young" and "little." One is said to have been twelve years of age.

Little children may *suffer*. "Man is born to trouble as the sparks fly upwards ;" and he very soon begins to feel it. The first noise a child makes is a cry. We have to wait for some things that we are born to

a long time, and sometimes they never come at all.
But the inheritance of sorrow we can soon call our
own.

Man was not made by God, in the first place, a
sorrowful creature. He was made good and happy,
and put into a beautiful garden, where the birds sang
sweetly, and the flowers bloomed with colours the most
lovely, and all kinds of pleasant fruits grew of their
own accord. And, what was best of all, God was
man's friend, and talked with him, and let him do
anything he liked, except sin. But man was not content with all that. He wanted to do the very thing,
and the only thing, he might not do. And since then,
the world has been full of all sorts of pain and grief.
And that is why children are so often in trouble.

These four children were sufferers in *different ways*.
Two of them were sick, and two of them were possessed by devils. Wicked spirits had been let to enter
them, and have power over both their minds and
bodies. One was "grievously vexed with a devil,"
and the other had "a dumb spirit" which took him
and tore and injured him many ways, casting him into
the fire and the waters.

There is scarcely anything more sad than to see
children sick, to see them in pain, to hear their cries
for relief, and behold the tears of distress running
down their little cheeks. And when they are too

young to tell where and what they suffer. And sometimes nothing can be done to help and soothe them.

But it is far worse when *Satan* is let to get hold of
children, and make their minds and hearts ill and
sick. Most people think that there is nothing, now,
like what we read of in the Gospels about devils getting into people, and making them mad. But whether
there is or not, we know from the Bible that devils
may enter people's *souls*, and make them love and do
what is wrong. Jesus Christ said that the Jews who
hated him were the children of the devil. Peter asked
Ananias why "Satan had filled his heart to lie." The
devil put it into the heart of Judas Iscariot to betray
Christ. And we read of persons who are "led captive
by the devil at his will." And the more we do what
we know to be wrong, the more likely we are to get
under the power of the devil, for all sins are the
" works of the devil." There are many people living
who have made themselves the slaves of Satan by in-
dulging their evil passions, " the lusts of the flesh and
of the mind," so that they are as much in his power
as the poor mad boy whose father so piteously asked
Jesus to help him.

One of these children was *dead*, when Jesus used
his power to save. When Jairus came to him about
her, she was at the point of death ; but when Jesus
came to the house, she was dead. Little children may

die. This child was only twelve years old ; but how
many children under that age are lying in the cold
and silent grave ? It is thought that *one half* of all
that are born die before they reach their twelfth birth-
day. Go into any grave-yard, and how often you read,
" Here lieth —— the infant son of ——." Yes, "the
grass withereth, the flower fadeth ;" the little blossoms
fall off and perish. And the prayers and breaking
hearts of fathers and mothers, and brothers and sisters, and friends and playmates, cannot stop children
dying. And all this is owing to that monster, *sin !*
" By one man sin entered into the world, and death
by sin," and " death reigned from Adam to Moses,
even over them that had not sinned after the simili-
tude of Adam's transgression."—Rom. v. 12, 14. And
death is reigning still. He is the "king of terrors,"
and there is no king that has so many subjects, and so
much power, or is so cruel in his rule.

The cases of these four children show us *how the
sorrow and sickness of children trouble others.* All of
them were brought under the notice of Jesus Christ
by either *father or mother.* And what distress they
show ! The nobleman cried out, " Come down ere
my child die." Jairus "besought him greatly" for his
daughter. The poor woman " cried after" him, and
" fell at his feet," and said, " Have mercy on me, O
Lord, thou Son of David ; my daughter is grievously

vexed with a devil." The father said, "Help *us*."
The mother said, "Have mercy upon *me*." See how
love binds parents and children together; makes children like parts of their parents. For good parents
feel towards their little ones as if they were their own
souls.

Ah! my children, you little know the love which
others feel for you. You cannot tell what care you
cost when too little to know of it. You cannot tell
the anxious hours spent in watching over you when.
sleeping in your tiny cots. You cannot tell the pain
felt through seeing you in pain ; and how often father
and mother would gladly have borne it all instead of
you, if they might. It was said to Mary, the mother
of Jesus, in reference to his sufferings, " Yea, a sword
shall pierce through thy own soul also ;" and every
woe that befalls your mind or body sends a pang to the
heart of those that love you. Should you not love,
and try to please them ? To disobey or grieve or
neglect kind parents is not only wrong in itself,
but it is *ungrateful ;* and ingratitude is the basest of
vices.

JESUS CAN HELP SUFFERING CHILDREN.

In all these cases Jesus was a very precious friend.
He saved these children from all the evils that afflicted

them. He cast out the devils from two. He cured one of a fever. And he raised the fourth from death to life.

What *power* there was in all this ! For it was done by *a word.* In two of the cases, Jesus was not present; and yet the children were made whole "the same hour" in which he spake. Diseases, death, devils, all fled at Christ's command. For he was a king, and "where the word of a king is, there is power." And he is a king now; and more a king than he was then. For then he was "poor and needy;" he was "despised and rejected of men ;" he was "a man of sorrows, and acquainted with grief." He was supported by charity; he had no home; and, when he died, he was laid in another man's grave. But now, "He is Lord of all." He is "crowned with honour and majesty." He "has all power in heaven and earth, that he should give eternal life to as many as God has given him."

Then Jesus *can* do anything that you can want or wish. I do not say that he *will,* but that he *can.* There is nothing in a child's heart that is too hard for him to do.

But we want more than power. We want *will* in a friend. It is useless to tell us that some one is *able* to do us good, if he is not willing. Children are often vexed when some unkind and rude companion teases

them by telling them he knows something they sadly
want to know, and could do something they sadly want
to be done; and yet refuses to tell it, or to do it.   I
dare say you have met with boys and girls who have
acted in this way, mocking you and laughing at your
trouble and vexation.   Jesus Christ does not annoy
people in this way.

He did not refuse *one* of these four prayers.   He
saved all four children.   He never refused any prayer
of distress.   Of all that came to him for themselves,
or for others, there was *not one* that went away without a blessing.   There have been many things said in
vain in this world, but no *true prayer* has ever been
said in vain.   There has not such a thing been known
since the world began, as a prayer not answered.
" For every one that asketh receiveth ; and he that
seeketh findeth; and to him that knocketh it shall
be opened."—Matt. vii. 8, 11.   You know how ready
your parents are to give you what is good for you.
Well, Jesus says, " If ye, being evil, know how to
give good gifts unto your children, how much more
shall your Father which is in heaven give good things
to them that ask him ?"

" Good things," not bad things.   Children often ask
and cry for things that they would like because they
are sweet and pleasant ; but they would not be good
for them.   If parents always gave their children what

they wished, they would kill them, or make them very ill and wretched. It is then kind to say, "No." God sometimes says, "No." But when he does so, it is because he loves us. He is wiser than we are, and can tell what would hurt us. If we *believed* that things would hurt us, and thought of it, we should not ask for them. God knows that, and therefore sometimes he refuses us. Like children, for "men are but children of a larger growth," we are perhaps cross and sulky at not having our own way; but we get to see that it is all right, and we are glad of it, afterwards. Paul had a very sharp and painful trouble, which he called "a thorn in the flesh."—2 Cor. xii. 7, 9. You have had thorns in the flesh, and you know what a keen pain they give. Well, Paul's trouble was like that. No wonder he asked Jesus Christ to take it out, asked it again and again; but he would not take it out. But he did better. He said, "My grace is sufficient for thee: for my strength is made perfect in weakness." And Paul was very glad that his prayer was not heard.

We learn another thing, *that Jesus Christ makes it a great matter that those who want him to do anything for them should trust in him.* The nobleman "believed the word that Jesus had spoken unto him." Jairus said, "Come and lay thy hands on her, that she may be healed; and she shall live." To the Syrophenician woman Jesus exclaimed, "O woman, great is thy faith : be it unto thee even as thou wilt." And to the father of the mad boy he said, "If thou can'st believe, all things are possible to him that believeth." Indeed, Christ always required faith in those who wanted any blessing of him.

And he does still. We cannot be *saved* without faith, for "by grace are ye saved through faith." We cannot be *holy* without faith, for God "purifies the heart by faith." We cannot *pray* rightly without faith, for "he that cometh to God must believe that he is, and that he is the rewarder of them that diligently seek him." We cannot *fight* against a wicked world without faith, for "this is the victory that overcometh the world, even our faith." We cannot *live* at all a spiritual life without faith, for, says Paul, "The life which I live in the flesh I live by the faith of the Son of God who loved me and gave himself for me."

We all like to be trusted. And so does Jesus Christ. He likes people to trust in his power and goodness. He has not promised to give us riches and health and honour, or even life ; and, therefore, we have no right to expect them ; but he has promised to give us what is *good and needful* for us, and therefore we should feel quite certain that he will do so. And he has promised to give what is wanted by the soul, if we seek it properly. He has promised to forgive our sins, and to teach us his blessed will, and to make us good ; and we must ask these things, believing that we shall have them, and we shall have them.

Jesus loves faith so much that he *tries it*, in order to bring it out, and make it stronger. Peter says that "the trial of faith is much more precious than of gold that perisheth, though it be tried with fire." Jesus Christ thought so too, and, therefore, tried the faith of those who came to him. He tried the woman of Canaan so. When she first spoke, "he answered her not a word." And, twice after, he seemed to deny her prayer. But she went on, in spite of all, and was blessed at last. Your parents sometimes do the same thing. When they mean to say "Yes," they sometimes keep you waiting just to see what you will say, and to prove that you are in earnest. And if we really want anything of men or God, the less we seem to get, the harder we should work, and, like blind Bartimœus, we should "cry the more a great deal.'

I have only one thing more to say. When Christ blessed these four children, it was *because of the prayers of others*. In three cases, the father prayed, and, in one case, the mother prayed. Oh ! it is a joyful truth, that we can pray for one another. We

are told to do so   And God has given us many instances of people who did so, and were heard. Parents
may pray for children, and children for parents, and
brothers and sisters for one another, and so on all
round the world !

But if Christ heard people for others *how much
more will he hear them for themselves ?*   My dear
children, do you ever pray for yourselves ?   Remember that the prayers of others will not get you saved,
unless you pray.   God may save one because others
pray for him, but he will not save him without his
own prayers.   "Every man shall bear his own bur-
den."   "Every one of us shall give account of himself
to God."   And if all the saints on earth, and all the
angels in heaven, were to pray for us, unless we prayed
for ourselves, and prayed believing, we could not pos-
sibly be saved.

CHRIST GIVING LIFE AND HEALTH TO CHILDREN.

He made the raging fever fly,
Just like some coward enemy ;
He raised again the little dear
Whose bed had just become her bier ;
He bade the demon-powers depart
That put a spell on mind and heart.

He did it all with but a word,
His work was done, when that was heard ;
Nor made it any difference where
That word was uttered, far or near ;
He spoke, and in that " very hour"
The sufferer felt his healing power.

O Lord, my woes are greater far
Than fever, death, or madness are ;
Yet, at thy word, they too will fly :
In mercy hear my humble cry ;
Bid me to live, my passions cool,
And send the demons from my soul.

Father and mother came to thee,
And said, O help my child and me !
And thou wilt hear me for another :
Bless me in parent, sister, brother ;
May they be thine, O Lord, and make
Them dear to me for thy dear sake

G

CHAPTER VIII

CHRIST'S REIGN, A BLESSING TO CHILDREN.

Isaiah xi. 6, 8.—"THE WOLF ALSO SHALL DWELL WITH THE LAMB; AND THE LEOPARD SHALL LIE DOWN WITH THE KID; AND THE CALF AND THE YOUNG LION AND THE FATLING TOGETHER; AND A LITTLE CHILD SHALL LEAD THEM. AND THE SUCKING CHILD SHALL PLAY ON THE HOLE OF THE ASP, AND THE WEANED CHILD SHALL PUT HIS HAND ON THE COCKATRICE' DEN."

THESE words are part of a very grand passage, which describes the nature and effects of the reign of Christ. You had better read with care from the first to the tenth verse. In the first part we are told what sort of a king is meant, the great gifts and powers which he would have. Then we are told of the way in which he would govern and judge men. And, lastly, we are told of the peace and happiness which the world would have when he ruled.

This last part is put in very *figurative* language. Perhaps you know what "figurative" means. A figure is when one thing is put for another, when one thing is called by the name of something else, which it is like. For instance. When a mother calls her babe "a pet lamb," that is a figure. She means that the child is to her like a lamb that is loved and fondled. When a man calls a boy "a dirty dog," he means that the boy has low and filthy actions, as a dog has. And when a good king is called "the father of his people," it means that he behaves like a father, that he does his best for the good of his people. All these are figures.

The three verses before us which speak of animals and serpents and children all being together like "a happy family," is full of figures. We are not to think that the time will ever come when the lower creatures will lose their tastes and habits, and the fierce and cruel and poisonous ones will become tame, and quiet, and harmless. God could make them so, if he liked; but he has not said that he does like.

Language like this is often used by the old poets to set forth the blessings of a just rule; and heathens who knew nothing of our Bible have said many things like this about "the golden age," which they looked forward to. Men who lived a very long time ago, and in countries a long way off, as Italy, Greece, and Persia, wrote something like this of Isaiah, only not so good. And they did not mean that animals would be changed. If you look at the *ninth* verse, you will see the *cause* of all this : "For the earth shall be full

of the knowledge of the Lord, as the waters cover the
sea." Now, *that* could not alter the animals. *Knowledge*, religious knowledge, changes *men*, not animals.
You can't make lions and leopards, and asps and
basilisks, gentle and safe for children to play with, by
teaching them about God. Isaiah meant that *the passions of men* would be subdued and changed. It is a
picture of peace and love.

JESUS CHRIST IS A KING.

There is no doubt that the prophet meant Jesus
Christ here. He is "the rod out of the stem of Jesse,
and the branch out of his roots." The apostle Paul
quotes part of this passage, in reference to Jesus
Christ, "Esaias saith, There shall be a root of Jesse,
and he that shall rise to reign over the Gentiles; in
him shall the Gentiles trust."—Rom. xv. 12.

Jesus Christ is a king. It was foretold that he would
be one. See Psalms xlv., and lxxii., and Isaiah xxxii.
And, when before Pilate's bar, he spoke of himself as
one. Although poor and weak, and without friends,
for his apostles had fled, and Judas had betrayed him,
and Peter had denied him, he yet used the words,
"My kingdom."

But his kingdom is of a very peculiar kind. He
has all things under his power. He can make nature,

and man, and devils do his will, even *against* their wills. But his glory, as a king, is that he can make people *willing* to obey and serve him. David sang of him, "Thy people shall be willing in the day of thy power"—shall be *volunteers.* They shall serve of their own accord.

This is a grand thing. One act done with a ready mind is worth ten thousand acts done against the will. And one willing servant is better than ten thousand unwilling slaves. Indeed, when a man acts against his will, *he* cannot be said to act at all; for the man is the will, not the hands. Jesus Christ thinks more of reigning over one who loves him and delights in his service than he does of reigning over all the devils in hell.

And this, as I have said, is the glory of his kingdom. He can make men love him. He can change their minds and hearts. He can turn enemies into friends, and rebels into loyal subjects. It was the complaint of a heathen who lived very long ago, "We can make laws, but we cannot make men obey them." This is the reason why there have to be so many police-men and soldiers, and judges and juries, and so many prisons. It is because human kings reign *over* men, not *in* them. But Jesus Christ reigns in them. He puts his throne in the heart. "The love of Christ constrains us."

Isaiah says that Christ shall reign by means of *knowledge*: "the knowledge of the Lord shall cover the earth." That is why "they shall not hurt nor destroy in all his holy mountain." And so we read in John's Gospel, "Pilate said unto him, Art thou a king, then ? Jesus answered, Thou sayest that I am a king. To this end was I born, and for this cause came I into the world, that I should bear witness unto the truth. Every one that is of the truth heareth my voice." Men often rule by fraud and falsehood. They build their power upon lies, and vain promises, and deceitful pretences. Jesus Christ never deceives people. He never did when he was here, and lost multitudes of disciples by it. And now his kingdom grows by convincing people of the truth, and persuading them to do what is right. His Holy Spirit opens the eyes of the mind, and in that way moves the affections. And when they are moved, there is pleasure in serving him. We "do the will of God from the heart."

The kingdom of Jesus is to become *greater and greater, until all obey him.* "Of the increase of his government and peace there shall be no end." Read Isaiah ix. 6, 7 ; and 1 Cor. xv. 24—28. It is true that now we "see not yet all things put under him," but he is "set down on the right hand of God, from henceforth expecting till his enemies be made his footstool "

"There is a good time coming," as the people sing. The Bible promises a season when Jesus shall reign over the whole earth. Then " the idols he will utterly abolish." Jew and Gentile will be as sheep in one fold, under one shepherd. Satan will be bound. Men will "learn war no more." " All shall know the Lord from the least even unto the greatest." God will dwell with men on the earth. All " men shall be blessed in him ; all nations shall call him blessed." And "the whole earth shall be filled with his glory." Then our text will be *a fact*. But, so far as Christ reigns, now, it is a fact. In every nation, in every house, in every heart, his blessed rule brings joy, and righteousness, and peace.

Look at the reign of Jesus Christ IN CONNECTION WITH LITTLE CHILDREN.

I have said that the meaning of the words is, that *men who are like wild beasts shall become tame and quiet.* Their rough and cruel passions shall be subdued. Love shall take the place of hate and revenge ; peace shall take the place of war. " The fruit of the Spirit is love, joy, peace, long-suffering, gentleness, goodness, faith, meekness, temperance."—Gal. v. 22, 23. " Put on therefore as the elect of God, holy and beloved, bowels of mercies, kindness, humbleness of

mind, meekness, long-suffering ; forbearing one another, and forgiving one another, if any man have a
quarrel against any : even as Christ forgave you, so
also do ye. And above all these things put on charity,
which is the bond of perfectness. And let the peace of
God rule in your hearts, to the which also ye are called
in one body ; and be ye thankful."—Col. iii. 12—15.

Wherever there are these graces, there will *little
children be blessed.* The Spirit of Jesus in men will
make them feel and act towards children as he did.
The charity and kindness which he puts into the heart
will be shown most to the most innocent and helpless.
Although most people have "natural affection," yet
there are countries where little children are cruelly
treated still. Indeed, we read every day of persons
in England who beat and starve them shamefully.
But where Christ reigns, there are good fathers and
mothers, and brothers and sisters, and neighbours and
masters. Christ said to Zacchæus, "This day is salvation come to *this house.*" And Paul and Silas said
to the Philippian jailor, "Believe on the Lord Jesus
Christ, and thou shalt be saved, and *thy house.*" Yes,
Christ saves *the house.* He blesses the family. And
little children have most reason to be glad of that, for
they feel it most.

But Christ's reign blesses children *by making them
good,* as well as by making others good.

They shall still *"play."* Zechariah says, "The
streets of the city shall be full of boys and girls playing." Many people think that religion makes men
gloomy and miserable. *It ought not to do it.* If it
does, it is men's own fault. If the light pains the eye,
it is because the eye is weak. "Wisdom's ways are
ways of pleasantness, and all her paths are peace."
"The kingdom of God is righteousness and peace, and
joy in the Holy Ghost." Good children ought to play
with more lightness of heart than other children, because they ought to be more happy.

But Christ, by making children good, *makes other
things more good to them. Beasts* are not to be changed
in their natures, but much of what *we suffer from beasts
is our own fault.* If they are kindly treated, they
lose much of their fierceness. The apostle James says,
"Every kind of beasts, and of birds, and of serpents,
and of things in the sea, is tamed, and hath been
tamed of mankind." No doubt the wildest and most
dangerous animals have been brought into subjection
by wise and gentle means. But what I mean, now,
is that we often provoke them, teaze and vex them ;
and children do so more than men. We have known
children who took a pleasure in tormenting poor animals, and who have suffered from it. Men become
angry and violent, when they are hurt and starved
and confined ; and we cannot expect animals to have

milder tempers than men. But kindness begets kindness even in the lower creatures; and it is true in
this as in other things, that "blessed are the merciful,
for they shall obtain mercy."

If religion does not make children kind to animals,
it does but little for them. A cruel child is a bad
child, and will very likely grow up to be a bad man.
Nero, the tyrant, when a child, loved to torment flies.
But a child that cares for the happiness of the creatures beneath him will care for the happiness of his
fellow-creatures, and become a thoughtful and merciful man.

I like to see in children a love of animals. It is a
good training for after life. The greatest and best
men have had their "pets." The Apostle John, we
are told, kept a tame partridge. It is to many a
source of great pleasure. Some children have got so
endeared to members of the brute creation as to feel
for them as companions, and to form ties of affection
with them like those between friends. And with
children it does not matter so much that animals
cannot talk, and know little. But perhaps they
know more than we think. At any rate they know
when they are treated kindly, and they know how to
return it. And this joy is greater because Jesus is king.

If children are made good, *men* will be better to
them. Bad children get into trouble. They get dis-

liked and beaten and shunned. There is nothing more disagreeable than bad children. Pride, obstinacy, ill-temper, passion are offensive in all; but they are most so in the young, because they are opposed to what is natural as well as what is right. But meek and modest and loving children will be dear to all. The rough and rude will not be rough and rude to them. The soft word of a child has often calmed a passionate father, who would have been worse for resistance or rebuke. Men who have been known not to fight at all have sometimes been safe when others have suffered loss. So that when Jesus reigns in children's hearts, the world is better to them. The beasts lie down with them.

But there are *evil things*, as well as evil men, and wild beasts, in the world; and Jesus makes *them* different by making us so. God does not order it so that good people shall not suffer like other people. They are sick, and poor; they have distress of mind; and they die. And you may say that troubles are like wild beasts and serpents. They come with great force, and great subtilty. Things bright as the serpent's skin, and handsome as the lion's or leopard's limbs, have often their teeth, and their sting. Disease and death are wolves and bears; but if we love Jesus, we may be at peace with them. Pleasure is a basilisk, but if we love Jesus, we may play with it. If Christ

the king, who is "Lord of all," rules us by his grace,
we need not fear them. Trouble will be our Father's
rod to correct our faults, and death our Father's servant to take us home.

THE GROUP OF GRACES:

A PICTURE AND A PUZZLE.

"The fruit of the Spirit is love, joy, peace, longsuffering, gentleness, goodness, faith, meekness, temperance."—GAL. v. 22, 23.

I lighted on a village green,
And saw a most delightful scene ;
A crowd of children full of cheer,
Assembled for amusement there.
Some played in groups, some singly played,
But what a stir and noise they made !

Yet most of all was I impressed
By some not mingling with the rest.
They seemed more thoughtful and more fair
Than common children often are ;
And, spite of varied form and face,
I thought a likeness I could trace.

The oldest, judging from his size,
A lad of large, expressive eyes,
With telescopic glass in hand,
Which could the glorious view command,
Appeared to find a pleasure rare
In bringing distant objects near.

The youngest, on its nurse's knee,
Looked slily up with chuckling glee ;
Then hid it in its nurse's breast,
As if to say, " Now come in quest ;"
Or pressed its lips upon her face,
And kissed her with a fond embrace.

The strongest, with a sturdy frame,
And thoughtful brow, well used to tame
His will, appeared resolved to find
Some problem which perplexed his mind ;
And thus, on self-improvement bent,
The quiet hours of evening spent.

There passed a ragged, crippled boy
Who stopped and heaved a heavy sigh :
One little girl, too full to speak,
But with a tear upon her cheek,
Begged him accept her tiny store,
And only wished that it was more.

One had a lamb which she caressed,
Squeezing it to her tender breast ;
She seemed a most bewitching child,
And when she caught my eye, she smiled ;
And to my question, in a tone
So sweet, replied, " It is my own."

A girl of very tender years
Went near the crowd, but soon in tears
Returned : a boy, as rude as strong,
Had struck her ; well she bore the wrong ;
And, sobbing for a while with pain,
She soon was calm, and smiled again.

Placed in a chair beneath a tree,
Sat, well content to hear and see,
A pallid invalid and lame,
Who ne'er had joined a merry game :
I spoke a word of sympathy ;
He said, " It is as it should be."

A fragile form, with placid mien,
Lay on a bank of mossy green,
Turning sometimes a clear blue eye
Towards the things of earth and sky ;
But finding mostly what she sought
Within the sphere of quiet thought.

The noisiest member of the group
Trundled with all his might a hoop;
A chubby, rosy, reckless thing,
That made the neighbouring wood to ring
With such a clear melodious voice,
That none could hear and not rejoice.

I left the scene; but oft since then
My thoughts have wandered back again.
And, though so much was pleasant there,
Still chiefly to that group repair;
That group will in my memory be
Through time, perhaps through eternity.

CHAPTER IX

CHRIST AND THE CHILDREN'S BREAD.

John xxi. 15 —"He saith unto him, Feed my lambs."

THIS was said to Peter. He had done very wrong, and sadly grieved Jesus Christ. After promising to be faithful to him, in all cases, though the rest of the apostles should fail, and in spite of loud warnings, he fell into the terrible sin of denying Jesus Christ again and again, and with oaths and curses.

He was rash. He had too much confidence in his own power. He thought too well of his love to Jesus. He did not expect what took place, and therefore did not know how much his faith would be tried. Solomon says, "He that trusteth in his own heart is a fool," but "blessed is the man that feareth always." And Jesus said, about this very time, "Watch and pray that ye enter not into temptation."

Peter sinned more than others; but he was not so bad as he appeared. If he had run away with the rest, he would have escaped the trial that made him fall. It was because "he followed Jesus," though "afar off," that he denied him. He was braver than the other apostles, went further into the fight, and so was wounded. We cannot tell what people are from seeing merely what they do. We must know what they have to bear, and to resist; and know what others have also.

> What's done we partly may compute,
> But know not what's *resisted*.

With all Peter's faults, he loved Jesus, and knew it. He was not ashamed to say so, even to Jesus himself, when he was questioned. He could appeal to Jesus about it. "Lord, thou knowest that I love thee." Jesus said, "Feed my lambs."

This was Peter's restoration to his office. By his great and public fall, he had lost that office, but Christ restored him. Judas, who sold Jesus, was lost, and went to his own place, because he never loved Jesus, and he sinned with thought and purpose and habit. But Peter did love Jesus, and his fall came from temptation, and sudden fear. And so Jesus put Peter again in the place he was in before.

When Jesus said to Peter, "Feed my lambs," he meant *little ones*. He might have called all his disciples lambs, but he did not do so now; for just afterwards he said, "Feed my sheep," thus marking them off into two classes.

H

WHAT IS MEANT BY FEEDING THE LAMBS?

There is nothing more important in a shepherd's task than *feeding* his flock. It is sometimes mentioned as if it took in *all* his work. No doubt it is so in the text. We cannot think Peter was to do nothing else than "feed the church of God." It means that he was to do all that a shepherd does to his sheep; watch, guide, rule, wash, and heal them, as well as give them food. But we often, when speaking of men's duties, mention one instead of all, the greatest one. We call one man a "ruler," though he does more things than rule. We call another man a "physician," though he does more things than order physic. But these are the principal things they do. So, "he shall feed his flock like a shepherd" means that he shall be a shepherd, and do all that shepherds do to their flocks.

However, let us speak now about feeding.

To feed the *body* is to give it that which it can use in the way of nourishment. Food helps the body by being changed into body. What we eat and drink is good so far as it can be turned into flesh and blood, and bone and muscle. Poison cannot be so turned. There is nothing for it to do. It is in the wrong place. The body does not like it, and tries to get rid of it; hence pain, and disease, and death. But good food undergoes a great change; and we become stronger and larger. For there is a constant waste going on in our bodies, and, in the course of a few years, every bit of our bodies is new. So that if it were not for food, which is always mending and repairing them, they would be in a sad way.

Now, the *soul* is very like the body in many things. And it is so in this. The life of the spirit is kept up like the life of the flesh. What Peter calls "the hidden man of the heart" needs food as much as the outward man of the body. But the food must be of another kind. It must be suitable to that which it is meant to nourish. The body, made of matter, must have food made of matter ; spirit must have spiritual food.

The food of souls is *truth*, and especially truth about *God*, his character, his will ; what he has done, and intends to do. "As new born babes, desire the sincere milk of the *word*, that ye may grow, if so be ye have tasted that the Lord is gracious." The life of the heart is in right thoughts and feelings and wishes, leading to holiness of conduct. And these must be fed by the things God has said in the Bible. "Thy words were found, and I did eat them," said Jeremiah. "I have esteemed the words of his mouth more than my necessary food," were Job's words. And so we read in the New Testament of being "nourished up in the words of faith and of good doctrine," and of " the wholesome words of the Lord Jesus."

But the food of the soul is more particularly the truth about *Jesus Christ himself*. He spoke, on one occasion—John vi. 35—45—at great length, of himself as the nourishment of men. "I am the bread of life : he that cometh to me shall never hunger ; and he that believeth on me shall never thirst." "Whoso eateth my flesh, and drinketh my blood, hath eternal life." Of course, it does not mean that we can do this in the same way that we can eat and drink other things. For Jesus Christ has no flesh and blood now. His is a "spiritual body." "Flesh and blood cannot inherit the kingdom of God," to which he has gone. But when Christ used those words he also said, "It is the spirit that quickeneth ; the flesh profiteth nothing : the words that I speak unto you, they are spirit, and they are life." It is *faith* that so receives Christ that the soul is nourished. He "dwells in the heart by faith." "The life we live is by the faith of the Son of God who loved us, and gave himself for us." Wonderful shepherd, not only to feed us, but to feed us with himself !

Now this truth, this truth about himself, is given to children. The Bible has "milk for babes." The spirit of God teaches the very young. Of course they can know very little in the way in which men can know things. They can have but small learning, and think but small thoughts. But the knowledge of

Jesus Christ does not depend on much learning and large thoughts. "At that time Jesus answered and said, I thank thee, O Father, Lord of heaven and earth, because thou hast hid these things from the wise and prudent and hast revealed them unto babes. Even so, Father ; for so it seemed good in thy sight." —Matt. xi. 25, 26.   And when a child is thus taught of God he can say with David, " I have more understanding than all my teachers, for thy testimonies are my meditation.   I understand more than the ancients, because I keep thy precepts."—Ps. cxix. 99, 100.

IT WAS A CHARGE TO PETER THAT HE SHOULD FEED CHRIST'S LAMBS.

God *employs men* as much as he can in building up his church.   I have told you why in the *fifth chapter.* When Jesus Christ did his mighty works on earth, works that men could not do, and could not help to do, Jesus Christ found a way to use his apostles and other men.   There are several instances in connection with children.   Jairus, the ruler of the synagogue, had a daughter twelve years of age, who had died, and Jesus Christ raised her to life again, and she walked : but "he commanded that something should be given her to eat."   Men could not give the child *life,* so he gave it.   But they could give her *food,* so

he ordered them to do it. He could have raised her
so that she should not want food, or should not want
it then : but he told others to feed her. On two
occasions, he fed thousands of men, " besides women
and *children*," by a miracle. But on both, he employed his apostles to carry the bread to the people.
He could have taken away their hunger without bread,
or have placed the bread before them at once, if he
had chosen ; but he did not like to do so. He did
what he only could do, and ordered men to do what
was within their power. He could have made us all
so as not to want food ; but he has pleased so to make
us that we have to work to feed ourselves, and one
another.

In feeding *souls*, Jesus Christ employs men. Men
cannot give spiritual life, any more than animal life ;
so he gives it. But men can use means ; men can
provide truth ; they can teach, persuade, and warn.
Christ is " *the chief* shepherd," as Peter calls him ;
but he has a great many *under-shepherds*, to whom he
says, " Feed the flock of God," " Feed my sheep,"
" Feed my lambs."

I cannot tell you all the ways in which Jesus Christ
uses men in feeding his flock. But let me mention
two or three.

He used men to *give us the Bible.* He could have
given it to us himself, but he chose rather to tell men

what to write, and they wrote "as they were moved
by the Holy Ghost." Great men, you know, instead
of writing their own letters, often have clerks and
secretaries to whom they say what they wish to be
written, and they write it; and, instead of telling
every man by himself what he thought and wished,
God disposed many men to write, and put into their
minds what to write, and so at last the Bible was
made. And the Prophets and Apostles, through the
Bible, are teaching and "feeding the church of God,"
to-day, and will feed it to the end of the world.

Christ uses men in the way of *teaching and preaching*. Every true minister is a shepherd. "Pastor"
is one of his names. And, as a shepherd who neglected his lambs would be a very bad shepherd, so a
minister who does not care for children is a very bad
minister. And none can have a title more sweet or
more worthy than "a teacher of babes."

But it is not ministers only that have to feed the
lambs. "Minister" means "servant," and there are
many who serve besides those who are set apart to do
it in a particular way. *Parents* are to "bring up
their children in the nurture and admonition of the
Lord." And wherever there is the same "mind that
was in Christ Jesus," there will be his love of children,
and his desire to do them good.

But we must not forget *the way in which Jesus*

Christ thinks of the feeding of the lambs. He thinks very much of it. It is not a little thing, that he does not much care whether it is done or not.

Look here. *Jesus Christ told Peter to do it.* Peter is called "the first;" and, though he was not what some make him to be, he was the leader and spokesman of the Apostles. An Apostle might think himself honoured by this task. And no wonder, for Christ did it himself; and "the disciple is not above his master, nor the servant above his lord."

And Jesus tells him to do it *first of all.* He says, "Feed my lambs," and afterwards, "Feed my sheep." The young go before the old in nature. The young prepare for the old. If one of these classes had to be left out, it would be better to leave out the old, and to choose the young.

And he would not put Peter to this task again, *till Peter had declared his love.* No one is fit to feed Christ's lambs who does not know and love the shepherd.

They are *Christ's lambs*—"my lambs." He made them, he died for them, he watches over them, and will not have them neglected or offended by any one, on pain of death.

CHRIST AND THE CHILDREN'S BREAD.

Very soon our flesh would die,
  But for daily bread,
Which the Father doth supply,
  So that we are fed.

And the spirit also lives
  On its proper good,
Which the Saviour kindly gives,
  For his truth is food.

Little children cannot eat
  All that others can ;
And the Saviour suits his meat
  Both to child and man.

He hath many to impart
  What they cannot make,
And with wise and loving heart
  Help them to partake.

Give me, Lord, an appetite
  For the bread of heaven,
May I take with great delight
  What thy love hath given.

CHAPTER X

CHRIST'S TENDER TREATMENT OF CHILDREN.

saiah xl. 11.—"HE SHALL GATHER THE LAMBS WITH HIS ARM, AND CARRY THEM IN HIS BOSOM."

THERE is not in the Bible any figure more full of truth and beauty than that of the shepherd. God was very fond in the Old Testament of calling himself the shepherd of good men. See how delightfully he is so described in the *Twenty-third Psalm.* And Jesus Christ, in like manner, spoke of himself at great length as a shepherd in the *Tenth chapter of the Gospel by John.*

Shepherds appear from that chapter, and from the accounts of travellers, to be very different in the East from what they are among ourselves. With us, a shepherd is simply a watchman, taking charge of his flock, and knowing them only as so many animals worth so much money. But, in the East, he is more like the friend of the sheep. Christ speaks of "the good shepherd" as knowing his own sheep, and as being known by them ; as calling them by their names; as being followed by them ; and as risking his life in seeking them when lost, or defending them when attacked.   And he says that in these respects he is a shepherd, and true Christians are his sheep.

"He shall feed his flock like a shepherd : he shall gather the lambs with his arm, and carry them in his bosom, and shall gently lead those that are with young." Jesus Christ is intended by these words. Let us dwell a little on them, so far as they belong to children.

SEE THE TENDERNESS OF JESUS CHRIST.

What a picture of loving, thoughtful care.   And Jesus Christ is *very tender*.   Men are sometimes very good, but at the same time hard and severe.   They would not do a wrong thing on any account, and yet they are not loved.   Their friends respect them, but do not love them.   Their children obey them, but do not love them.   Paul speaks of such—"Scarcely for a righteous man will one die, yet peradventure for a good man some would even dare to die."

. Jesus Christ is not like these.   "I beseech you," says Paul, "by the *meekness* and *gentleness* of Christ." And Isaiah—xlii. 2, 3—wrote of him, "He shall not cry, nor lift up, nor cause his voice to be heard in the street. A bruised reed shall he not break, and the smoking flax shall he not quench." He says himself, "Take my yoke upon you, and learn of me : for I am meek and lowly in heart."—Matt. xi. 29. Indeed, he is called "the Lamb of God," he is so gentle and pure. He is merciful ; and his is "tender mercy."

See the tenderness of Jesus SUITING ITSELF TO THE STATES AND WANTS OF HIS FLOCK.

A good shepherd does not treat all his sheep alike. That would be really to treat them differently, because they differ from one another, and need different treatment. You know it would never do for a doctor to give the same kind of medicine to all his patients ; or for a parent to feed and clothe all his children in the same way ; or for a teacher to make all his scholars learn the same lessons. Regard must be paid to age, power, and character.

So it is with a shepherd. A flock is made up of a number of sheep very unlike each other. Some are old, some are young. Some are strong, some are weak. Some are well, some are sick. Some have the use of all their limbs, some have suffered from accidents or violence, and are torn or lame. This was God's complaint against "the shepherds of Israel." " The diseased have ye not strengthened, neither have ye healed that which was sick, neither have ye bound up that which was broken, neither have ye brought again that which was driven away, neither have ye sought that which was lost."

Jesus Christ does all these things, and all other things needed by his flock. He knows them all, knows their hearts, and histories, and circumstances. In him all fulness dwells, all wisdom, power, and grace; and out of his fulness they all receive.

See the tenderness of Jesus in the way in which he suits himself to, and deals with, THE YOUNG.

He gathers and carries the lambs. That is, he remembers the young and feeble among his followers, and shows his kindness in the way in which he helps them on in the path of life and godliness.

Christians may be lambs for two reasons. They may be lambs because they are young in *years*, or because they are young in *grace*. There are two kinds of life that we can live. There is the natural life, the life of the flesh, which every one lives; and there is the spiritual life, the life of faith and love and obedience to God, which only Christians live. And as there are two lives, so there are two births, and two childhoods. The life of the spirit may begin in a man when the life of the flesh is young or is old ; and so the old man may be a young Christian ; and the young man may be by comparison an old Christian. The *lambs* take in all who are children, either in years or in grace ; and these Jesus gathers and carries ; that is, he deals with them *according to their needs.* The young are *weak.*   They cannot do or bear so much as the old.   Lambs soon get wearied and worn, and want to lie down, or fall behind ; and the tender shepherd bears them like an infant.   And Jesus Christ does likewise.   He deals with them so kindly that they do not suffer from being lambs.   In other words, he does not treat them as sheep, but as lambs.

He does so in *teaching* them.   There is a great difference between an infant-school, and a boys' school ; and a great difference between a school of any kind, and a college.   The lessons become more hard day by day.   The world was like an infant once, in knowledge and feeling ; and, when Moses was its schoolmaster, the things taught were very few and simple, and the teaching was chiefly by pictures.   But when the world got older, and Jesus Christ was the schoolmaster, the pictures were nearly all done away, and a great deal more was taught, "the whole counsel of God."   So when the Apostles were infants in religion, Christ said, " I have many things to say unto you, but ye cannot bear them now.   Howbeit when he, the Spirit of truth, is come, he will guide you into all truth."

The Bible has "milk for babes," and "strong meat" for men. Therefore the Psalmist said, "Thy testimonies are wonderful, therefore doth my soul keep them. The entrance of thy words giveth light, it giveth understanding unto the simple." The Bible is like the ocean, a feather may float on it, and Noah's Ark, or the Great Eastern, may sail on it. It has things too great for the wisest man to understand, and yet an infant may find the way of salvation.

Jesus Christ helps children by giving them *strength* according to their needs. We have not only to *learn*, but to *do*. Much that we learn at school has nothing to do with our conduct, but the Bible is given to us to show us how to *live*. Life is often called a "walk," and the Bible points out the way in which we should go, and gives us power to go in it. Children cannot walk at first; they fall in trying to walk, and hurt themselves. They have to learn, to be held by the hand; and, when they hurt themselves, they have to be made well again. So God said to the Jews of old, "I taught Ephraim also to go, taking them by their arms; but they knew not that I healed them." He taught them to walk when they were a young nation. He helped them; and when they hurt themselves, he made them well. And so David said of himself, "My soul followeth hard after thee; thy right hand upholdeth me."

We cannot do anything good without God's help. Our hearts have so much that is evil in them, and there is so much that is evil outside of them, that we should never do good at all, if God did not kindly assist us by his Spirit. Therefore Paul says, "Work out your own salvation with fear and trembling, for it is God that worketh in you both to will and to do of his good pleasure." And, as children are very weak, God gives them more strength. It is like holding them while they are learning to walk.

Jesus Christ is careful and loving to the young in *not requiring more of them than they are fit for.* It is a beautiful saying, that "God tempers the wind to the shorn lamb." He would be very cruel who set a man and a child the same task, or expected them both to carry the same weight. And so he would be a hard shepherd who made a sheep and a lamb walk the same distance.

Jesus Christ does not look for more from any man than is within his reach, than he knows enough to do, and is strong enough to do. He knows that children can do but little. And he only asks from them that which they can do. When they become wiser and stronger, he expects more from them, and puts more upon them.

What a blessed thing it is that God knows our bodies and our minds ; and what is, and what is not, possible for us. "God will not suffer us to be tempted above that we are able." "As thy day, so shall thy strength be."

Let not children be cast down and sad at seeing others do more than they themselves can do. It would be like a lamb mourning that it had not the strength of a sheep. Jesus Christ carries the lambs.

Lastly, the text is true in reference to the *comforts* which Jesus Christ gives to children. Men can take delight in things which give no pleasure to little ones ; and little ones are made glad by what cannot give joy to men. The "good shepherd" carries his lambs "in his bosom," where they are nice and warm.

Christ's comforts for the young suit their feelings, and their sorrows. Have you ever noticed how God likens himself to *fathers* and *mothers* in his love for his people ? Your warmest, sweetest thoughts are of the care and kindness of your parents. How they have granted your wishes ! How they have soothed your pains ! How they have wiped your tears ! Well, God says *he is like a father, and like a mother.* "Like as a father pitieth his children, so the Lord pitieth them that fear him." "As one whom his mother comforteth, so will I comfort thee."

"If there be any consolation in Christ," then, let little children be joyful. He is able to fill their young hearts with great gladness ; and if they seek him, he will do it.

I

THE LAMBS CARRIED.

Jesus is a Shepherd kind,
　Feeds, protects, and leads his sheep;
All who love him ever find
　He can keep as none can keep.

Jesus is both kind and wise;
　All his sheep his notice share;
But with special care he eyes
　Those who need a special care;

Gently leads the wearied dam,
　Gently binds the bruised limb;
And his bosom bears the lamb
　Like an infant dear to him.

He the simplest thoughts instills,
　He the mildest rules imparts,
Arms with power the weakest wills,
　Fills with joy the saddest hearts.

Who to him would trust a fold
　Who the lambs neglected sore?
Nor could Jesus love the old,
　If he loved not children more.

CHAPTER XI

CHRIST PLEASED WITH CHILDREN'S SONGS.

Matt. xxi. 15, 16. — "AND WHEN THE CHIEF PRIESTS AND SCRIBES SAW THE WONDERFUL THINGS THAT HE DID, AND THE CHILDREN CRYING IN THE TEMPLE, AND SAYING, HOSANNA TO THE SON OF DAVID; THEY WERE SORE DISPLEASED, AND SAID UNTO HIM, HEAREST THOU WHAT THESE SAY? AND JESUS SAITH UNTO THEM, YEA; HAVE YE NEVER READ, OUT OF THE MOUTHS OF BABES AND SUCKLINGS THOU HAST PERFECTED PRAISE."

JESUS CHRIST had just ridden into Jerusalem as a king. We do not read of his riding but once, and then it was upon a borrowed ass. It was not mean to ride upon an ass in Judæa, as it would be in England; but he must have been a poor king who had not one of his own. But Christ had nothing of his own; not even a home, or a tomb.

He was only accompanied by a few followers, mostly plain and poor men; and by a crowd of people who a few days afterwards shouted, "Crucify him, crucify him."

I should think there never was such an entry of a king into his capitol as this. Kings are glad and proud at such times; but Jesus "wept." Kings salute and thank the people; but Jesus bewailed the guilt and doom of the Jews. Kings give honours and

receive homage ; but within five days Jesus was to die
in that very city. Kings are attended by the chief
people in church and state ; but the chief people here
took no part in this scene, and were very angry with
those who did.

All this was because though Jesus was a king, he
was very different from other kings. "My kingdom is not of this world." "The kingdom of God
cometh not with observation." "The kingdom of
God is within you."

When Jesus came into the city, he went into the
temple of God, and cast out those who were making
it a place of trade, and healed the blind and the lame
who came to him. And then we are told, in the text,
that when the priests and the scribes, that is, those
who had to do with the service and law of God, saw
what he did, and heard the children shout "Hosanna
to the Son of David," they were very angry. But
Jesus was pleased, and defended the children, and
would not stop their joyful cry.

There are many things in this passage from which
we may learn wisdom.

LISTEN TO THE LITTLE CHILDREN SINGING CHRIST'S
PRAISE.

They were very *glad.* The people about them were
very glad. Nearly every one was in good humour

then. The reason was this : the people thought that Jesus was going to deliver them. The Jewish nation was now under the power of the Romans, and the people thought that Jesus would set them free. If we, the English nation, were under the power of the French, should we not be glad if any one came to set us free ? Jesus did not come to do that, but the Jews thought he would ; and while they thought so, they made a great deal of Jesus; and when they found that they were mistaken, they turned against him. When he rode into Jerusalem as a king, therefore, they were in high glee ; and the children were in high glee too, just because the men were.

We read that when the jailer at Philippi was con-verted, that is, was *turned* from being a bad man to be a good man, he brought Paul and Silas into his house, and set meat before them, and rejoiced, believ-ing in God, with all his house. It is not said that they believed, only that they rejoiced with him. It is very likely that little children were there who did not know exactly *why* he was so happy, but they were happy in seeing him happy.

We cannot help being moved by the feelings of those about us. If *they* are sad and gloomy, it makes us so, more or less ; and if they are full of joy and mirth, it cheers and arouses us. How careful this should make us, for the sake of those about us ! How important that we should try to be happy ourselves that we may have a happy influence upon them! If we can't help being sad, we should keep it in as much as possible. Jesus told his disciples that when they "fasted," they were to look cheerful, and "not of a sad countenance."

But these children shouted Hosanna, not only because they were glad along with others, but because *others had shouted it just before.* In the ninth verse it is said, "And the multitudes that went before, and that followed, cried, saying, Hosanna to the Son of David : Blessed is he that cometh in the name of the Lord ; Hosanna in the highest." When the children shouted the same thing, therefore, they only echoed the people's cry. They went on doing what had been done by others. They *imitated* them. None of the children understood what they did as well as the men ; and some of them understood nothing. But, whether they understood or not, they shouted because the men had just done it.

Children are fond of *imitating*, which means *copying*, what they see others do. It is one of the first things they do. Very tiny babies will copy the actions of parents and grandparents. They will put on their dress, sit like them, speak like them. This is called *mimicry*. Many of the *games* and *amusements* of children are copies of men's and women's actions.

Their dolls and dolls' houses, their guns and swords, their shops and chapels, are all of this kind. Jesus Christ took one of his figures or similes from this habit of children. He said, "Whereunto shall I liken this generation? It is like unto children sitting in the markets, and calling unto their fellows, and saying, We have piped unto you, and ye have not danced; we have mourned unto you, and ye have not lamented."—Matt. xi. 16, 17. That is, the Jews were *like children playing*, and turning sulky and perverse, so that nothing would please them.

But if children are so fond of imitating, of doing what others do, they should take care to be as much as they can with those who do only *what is worth being copied*. Multitudes have been ruined by bad examples. You have heard the proverb, "Example is better than precept." That is, when it is *good*. When it is *bad*, it is *worse*. There is another proverb like it, "Actions speak louder than words." Actions are more likely to be copied than words are to be attended to. And therefore the Bible says, "Follow not a multitude to do evil." In this matter we are something like sheep, a flock of whom will rush after one, without thinking at all where he is going to. "Be *followers* [imitators] *of God* as dear children." "Follow the Lamb withersoever he goeth."

LISTEN TO PRIESTS AND SCRIBES COMPLAINING OF THE CHILDREN.

They were "sore displeased." There were *two reasons* for this. They *hated Jesus Christ*, and therefore did not like any one not to hate him too. Matthew says, "When they saw the wonderful things he did." They were now plotting his destruction. They had already decided to kill him, and only waited for an opportunity to do it quietly, because they were afraid of. the people. And why? Because Christ would not do what they wanted him to do, and preached things they did not like. Christ was good, and they were bad; he loved God, and they hated him. They knew he was against them, because they were wrong. People often hate those who reprove them. It is very foolish. It is like hating the physician for ordering medicine. And for priests who had charge of divine service, and scribes who had care of divine law, to hate God's Son, was it not shocking?

As they hated Christ, they felt *condemned by these children for praising him*. This is one reason why people who are not good hate those who are. Perhaps you have sometimes felt a wrong feeling to other children who would not join you in what they did not think good. Has it not been because it was like saying that *you were wrong*? Of course, if we act unlike others, we say by our actions that they act amiss. So Noah is said, when he built the ark, to have "condemned the world." His "faith" condemned the world's unbelief. His "fear" condemned the world's ease and calm. And the world does not like to be condemned, does not like to be made to feel that it is wrong ; and therefore hates the righteous. When these Pharisees heard the children shout, they knew, whatever they might say, that they ought to be doing it themselves, and therefore tried to stop them.

But see how *cunning* they are ! It is said in this very chapter that "they feared the multitude, because they took him for a prophet." So they said to him, " Hearest thou what these say ?" So they had said to him before, "Master, rebuke thy disciples." They did not want to make a disturbance, but to get their will by quiet means. And then they managed to poison the people's minds against Jesus, and then they all put him to death.

In all ages, there have been great numbers of people who have tried to silence Christians, young or old. Sometimes they have killed them ; sometimes shut them up in prisons ; sometimes sent them into other countries, far away from friends and relatives. These things are not done so often now ; but wicked people still hate good people ; and wicked children hate good children, and hurt them and teaze them in many ways.

When these enemies of Christ said, "Hearest thou

what these say?" they felt contempt for the children and thought Christ would too. But they did not know him. Instead of blaming the children, he spoke well of them.

LISTEN TO JESUS DEFENDING THE CHILDREN.

"Jesus saith unto them, Yea; have ye never read, Out of the mouths of babes and sucklings thou hast perfected praise." Jesus 'quoted from the eighth Psalm ; but he did not mean to say that the writer of that Psalm was thinking of *these* children when he wrote ; but that they were doing *the same kind of thing* of which David spoke.

How different the same things are to different persons ! These men heard something offensive ; Jesus heard something pleasant. These men heard a thing to be stopped ; Jesus heard a thing to go on. And so it is always, what we hear and see gets a colour and a sound from our own thoughts and feelings.

These children did not know all that was meant by what they said. They—at least some of them—perhaps knew nothing. Christ does not think so much of what we know, as what we feel and do. He looks at the heart; and if that is right, he is pleased.

Christ will always defend those who love and praise him, in some way or other. He says of his sheep, and it takes in his *lambs*, "I give unto them eternal life, and they shall never perish."

CHILDREN SINGING HOSANNAS.

Listen to the merry ring
  Of the youthful crowd ;
Hear their little voices sing —
  Voices sweet and loud.

They have heard the shout of men
  Welcome David's Lord ;
Well may little children, then,
  Echo back the word.

Jesus loves that word to hear,
  Some in scorn oppose ;
It is music in his ear,
  Discord to his foes.

Even in these better days,
  There are hearts so wrong,
That they cannot bear his praise,
  Though in infant song.

But the Saviour will defend,
  Let who will assail ;
He's the little children's friend,
  And will never fail.

Let the Saviour's praise be sung
  With a joyful will,
And each childish heart and tongue
  Welcome Jesus still.

CHAPTER XII

CHILDREN BEFORE CHRIST'S GREAT WHITE THRONE.

Rev. xx. 11, 12.—"AND I SAW A GREAT WHITE THRONE, AND HIM THAT SAT ON IT. . . . AND I SAW THE DEAD, SMALL AND GREAT, STAND BEFORE GOD."

THIS is part of a description of the last judgment, the longest description, except one, that is to be found in the Bible. John had an image of the judgment in his mind. He "saw" it.

It is a very dreadful one. It is so dreadful that it is strange that any one can read it without trembling. Children are afraid when called up before a parent or a master, in the presence of others, to give an account of some small matter. What must it be to stand at the bar of God, along with all that ever lived, to be udged for our whole lives, with the heavens and the earth passing away, and the vast world of men and children divided into two great classes, the lost and the saved! "There is nothing awful but judgment."

I wish you to think of *one thing* about the judgment. I wish you to think of *Jesus Christ as judging children.*

There are many other things on which I might speak,
but this is most suitable and most important for you.

JESUS WILL BE THE CHILDREN'S JUDGE.

The text says that small and great stood "before
God." But we are to understand that Jesus Christ
will be the judge. There are several places where he
is so spoken of. He spoke so of himself, John v. 22
to 27 : " The Father judgeth no man, but hath committed all judgment unto the Son; that all men should
honour the Son, even as they honour the Father. For
as the Father hath life in himself, so hath he given to
the Son to have life in himself; and hath given him
authority to execute judgment also, because he is the
Son of Man." And if we needed anything more than
this, we have it in the account he gives us of the last
judgment, Matt. xxv. 31—46 : " When the Son of
Man shall come in his glory, and all the holy angels
with him, then shall he sit upon the throne of his
glory : and before him shall be gathered all nations :
and he shall separate them one from another, as a
shepherd divideth his sheep from the goats ; and he
shall set the sheep on his right hand, but the
goats on the left." So that the shepherd will be the
judge. This shows us who is meant when " the small
and the great" are said to " stand before *God*."

And is it not *fit* that Jesus should be judge? I do not mean because he is divine only. Of course he *is that*, or he could not be judge. A mere man could not judge the world. A mere man could not judge another man ; nor even himself. For, in order to judge a man, his thoughts and feelings must be known, and the motives of all his actions ; and, further, all his past history, and the whole of his circumstances, his privileges, and temptations, what he has been, and what he has not been, what he has done, and what he might have done. No man can know all this of himself or others. God puts together his knowledge of the heart, and his judgment of men,— Jer. xvii. 9, 10, "The heart is deceitful above all things, and desperately wicked ; who can know it? I the Lord search the heart, I try the reins, even to give every man according to his ways, and according to the fruit of his doings."

But Jesus is *human* as well as divine. And it is well that in "the man Christ Jesus," we should "stand before God." It is well that he who was so humbled should be so honoured. It is well that he who was "in the form of God," and was "obedient unto death," should be "highly exalted ;" and that at his "name every knee should bow." It is well that he who "tasted death for every man" should be "crowned with honour and majesty." If we feel with him in his shame and sorrow, shall we not rejoice with him in his glory ? We have grieved at his disgrace, shall we not be proud of his power and fame ?

Jesus Christ is judge. Surely it is good for man to think so. Of course there would have been no danger of wrong being done to any one, if the judge had not been man ; but, somehow or other, we have a feeling that makes the judgment less terrible when we think of a man being the judge. It is, in fact, not less terrible, but it *seems* so to us. When a foreigner is tried for a crime in an English Court of Justice, he is allowed to have half the jury made up of foreigners. This is meant both to make it sure that the person accused shall have a fair trial ; and that he and his countrymen shall feel that he has a fair trial; although foreigners often choose to be tried by Englishmen only. Now, when we know that "The world will be judged by *that man* whom God has ordained," our poor weak minds cannot help but be glad of the fact.

But how different he will appear as judge from what he appeared as saviour ! His first coming was in poverty and weakness and death ; his second coming will be in honour and majesty. His first was as an afflicted man, and a suffering servant; his second will be as the "Lord of all." At his first, he was attended by a few humble men ; at his second, he will be attended by "an innumerable company of angels,"

and "ten thousand of his saints." He will come "in
the clouds of heaven." He will "appear in flaming
fire." "He will come in his own glory, and in the
glory of the Father, and of the holy angels."

CHILDREN WILL STAND BEFORE THE JUDGE, JESUS
CHRIST.

" We must all appear before the judgment seat of
Christ, that every one may receive the things done
in his body, according to that he hath done, whether
it be good or bad." What an awful sight ! There is
nothing more awful than the sight of a large crowd.
Perhaps you have seen one ; perhaps you have been
placed, on some grand occasion, where you could see a
multitude of people, either in the streets, or in an open
space ; and you have felt very strangely and solemnly.
What must it be when all that are living through-
out the wide world, and all that have ever lived, are
brought together, and "small and great stand before
God ?"

Children will make a very large part of that vast
crowd. If you think of the families that you know,
you will see that there are, one with another, nearly
as many children as grown up people. Well, all the
children living when Christ comes, and all that have
died children during many thousands of years, will be
there.

And *they will be there to be judged.* A little way beyond our text, we read, "The books were opened," and "the dead were judged out of those things which were written in the books, according to their works." The thought expressed is this.   It is common for men to keep a record of the actions of those beneath them. Sometimes parents put down in a book the way in which their children behave.   And sometimes masters keep an account of the conduct of their servants. And, when there is cause for doing so, the books are opened.   So, although God does not keep account in books, it will be *as if he did.*   God often speaks of himself as doing what men do, to help us to understand him.   He even sometimes does what men do for this end.   Paul says that "an oath for confirmation is to men an end of all strife.   Wherein God, willing more abundantly to shew unto the heirs of promise the immutability of his counsel, confirmed it by an oath." And so here, and in many other places, he is spoken of as acting after the manner of men.

"According to their *works.*"   Christ will judge men by what they have done.   Not by what they say they are, nor by what they think they are, but by what they *do.*   There is no sign of what a man is like his *deeds.*   Solomon says, "Even a child is known by his doings, whether his work be pure."   But the deeds are not always things outside, and seen of men.   We do

J

a great deal in our hearts ; thoughts are deeds, desires are deeds ; and Christ knows them.

The deeds of men *are not the same.* We shall be judged by *our own* deeds. The small and the great are very unlike one another ; and Christ will not treat children as he will treat men. Very many children will not be able to give an account of themselves. They never knew good from evil. *We* do not know when children are old enough to have to answer for what they do, but Jesus Christ can tell.

Children will be judged *as children.* If you trusted another person with some money, you would expect that he would give you an account of the *exact sum* so entrusted to him ; not more, for that would not be just to *him* ; not less, for that would not be just to *you.* Jesus Christ says that he himself acts in this way. There are "few stripes" for some, and "many stripes" for others. "For unto whomsoever much is given, of him shall be much required : and to whom men have committed much, of him they will ask the more."

It would be very wrong to deal with children as with men. It would not be "judging the world in *righteousness.*" No ; Jesus will deal with the least just according to their real actions, and the real nature of them. He will make a difference between the younger and older, the weaker and stronger. He will

not try the child of a beggar as the child of a king.
He will not think the child of bad parents has as
much to answer for as the child of good parents. Thus
he will notice the distinction not only between children and men; but between some children and other
children.

THINK OF WHAT WILL FOLLOW THE JUDGMENT OF CHILDREN.

The fifteenth verse says, "whosoever was not found
written in the book of life was cast into the lake of
fire;" which teaches us, that there are *two classes;*
those who *are* written in the book of life, and will
therefore be saved; and those *not* written in the book
of life, and will therefore be lost. Christ said the same
thing. "And these shall go away into everlasting
punishment, but the righteous into life eternal."

I shall say but little about *the punishment.* It is
so dreadful a subject. And the Bible says so little
about it. But what it does say is of such a nature
that it is wonderful that any man should run the
least risk of being so punished. And yet there are
many, says Jesus, who do so. The worst thing we
know of, the most painful thing, is used to shew what
a terrible place hell will be. It is called "the lake of
fire." I cannot tell whether there will be any *real*

K

fire there, but there will be something *as bad*, or Christ would not have used the word.

Even *here*, men, and children too, have dreadful sufferings. God sends to them, in this world of mercy and salvation, great troubles and pains. What will he send them in a world of wrath, where he has given up all hope of doing them good? How much sometimes *the kindest human parent* will inflict of pain for children's faults, the faults of days, and hours. What, do you suppose, will be the punishment for the sins of *a life?* and sins committed against God, and against Christ?

There is an awful thought in our very subject: *Jesus Christ judging children.* The doom of every one will come from his lips. He will say "blessed" to some, and "cursed" to others; and the fact will make the reward of those more sweet, and the doom of these more painful. There is not a more awful word in the Bible than this, "the wrath of the *Lamb*." Just because the contrast is so great. A lamb is the emblem of meekness, gentleness, and patience; and if "the Lamb of God," the kind and tender Jesus, is angry and gives us up to sorrow and despair, there *can be* no hope.

But let us look at the brighter side. "Thy wrath is come, and the time of the dead, that they should be judged, and that *thou shouldest give reward unto thy servants the prophets, and to the saints, and them that*

fear thy name, small and great." It may seem curious
that we should speak of God's rewarding what any
poor, sinful creatures do ; but he speaks of it himself.
And it may seem still more curious that we should
speak of his rewarding what children do ; but Jesus
Christ says that he who gives "a cup of cold water"
to a disciple in his name shall not lose "his reward."
Now children can do *that,* and other things quite as
great, and greater, because they love him. If our
"hearts are right," all is right. The poor widow, who
gave but two mites, gave more than the rich men who
cast of their abundance into the treasury. That is,
not more *in itself,* but more *in proportion.* In this
way, Christ teaches us, a child may give more than a
merchant or a king ! And so, in like manner, a child
may *bear* more, and *do* more, as well as give more.

There will be little children in heaven. "Their
angels" are there, and they will be there. All children who have died before they knew what sin was will
be there ; and all children who have been sorry for
having sinned, and have asked God very earnestly to
forgive them for Christ's sake, will be there. And
heaven will be their *home.* Christ called it his
"Father's house." And it will be the house of all
God's "dear children." And they will be so happy
there! "For the Lamb which is in the midst of the
throne shall feed them, and shall lead them unto

living fountains of waters : and God shall wipe away all tears from their eyes."

"The small and great" will inherit life : and *children as such.* They will not be men and women in heaven at first, but children. What a blessed thing to grow to manhood *there;* like young plants taken from a common field and placed in a beautiful garden !

Children must not think that heaven is a place only for grown-up people. I am afraid that many children have heard heaven spoken of in such a way that they do not want to go there. They have been told that certain people will be there, and that certain things will be done there ; and as they do not like the people nor the things, they have rather a dread of heaven.

I knew a little girl who asked her mother if there would be "any pudding" in heaven. I should think it was not very likely, because I believe pudding will not be *wanted* there. But I am sure of this, that *if it were wanted*, if people could not be happy without it, God would provide it. But many things which we could not do without on earth, we shall not need in heaven. We could not do without the *sun*, nor without *places of worship*, on earth. The life of the body, and the life of the soul, would soon come to an end without these things. And yet there will be no sun and no temple in heaven. Christians will be so good, that all places will be alike holy ; and heaven will be so bright that even the sun will not be necessary.

But *all that children really want to make them happy will be there.* Parents on earth are wise to suit their pleasures to children of all ages, and God is wiser than any earthly parents. But we should not trouble ourselves by thinking what we want now; we should wait till we get to heaven, and then we shall find that God "will withhold no good thing" from us.

And heaven *will last for ever.* Our joy here is often sadly spoilt by the thought that it will be soon over. The sweet-meat, the game, the holiday, however nice, must come to an end. But this thought will never enter the minds of those who are saved. Every thing in heaven will go on for ever. "In God's presence is fulness of joy; at his right hand are pleasures for evermore.

Let every child that reads this book say, "I will make up my mind to go to heaven." Jesus Christ asks you to do it, and you cannot please him more than by doing it.

CHILDREN WITH CHRIST IN HEAVEN.

The saints shall all in heaven appear,
With Christ the Lord of all ;
The great, however great, be there,
The small, however small.

For Christ has good in ample store ;
  And long, hard lives are blest ;
While they who worked but one short hour
  Have payment with the rest.

He made our childish hearts, and knows
  How childish hearts to fill ;
And gladness from his presence flows
  A river, or a rill.

Children in heaven like lambs will play,
  Like plants will flourish well ;
It is their Father's house, and they
  Will with the Father dwell.

There will be little crowns so bright
  And songs so sweet to sing,
And harps of which with great delight
  A child may sweep the string.

But nothing in that holy place
  Will so the heart rejoice,
As to behold the Saviour's face,
  And listen to his voice.

He will my powers of joy increase,
  And all those powers supply
From springs whose waters never cease,
  With fruits that never die.

TO CHRIST.

Though but lambs, we yet have strayed ;
Worn, and weary, and afraid
               Of dangers sore,
We would come to thee to-day,
Heeding nought that whispers " Nay,"
                E'en for an hour.

Thou dost know the childish heart,
Thou dost act the Saviour's part ;
               Be thou our trust.
Through the scenes of all our life,
In the last and dreadful strife
                With death and dust.

More we need than open fold,
E'en a shepherd's help and hold,
            .   To come to thee ;
All that brings to thee is thine,
Christ alone to Christ can join ;
               Christ in us be !

Draw us by thy word and law,
By thy love and sorrows draw,
        And Spirits' breath;
By thy childhood and thy youth,
By thy manhood's right and truth,
        And glorious death.

Shepherd of thy chosen sheep,
Kindly heal and feed and keep
        By staff and rod ;
Soothe and succour in distress,
Lead us in thy righteousness
        Unto thy God.

Soon within the fold above
May we rest, and never rove,
        And never try ;
With no foes to hurt or frown,
And ourselves no more our own,
        Eternally.

A. Ireland & Co., Printers, Manchester.

.

www.ingramcontent.com/pod-product-compliance
Lightning Source LLC
Chambersburg PA
CBHW031157050726
47495CB00019B/2348